Ignite Your Spark

HOW TO FIND PURPOSE AND TAKE BOLD
ACTION TOWARDS YOUR DREAMS

Ignite Your Spark

HOW TO FIND PURPOSE AND TAKE BOLD
ACTION TOWARDS YOUR DREAMS

REBECCAH STATHAM

Dean Publishing
PO Box 119
Mt. Macedon, Victoria, 3441
Australia
deanpublishing.com

Copyright © Rebeccah Statham
All rights reserved. No part of this publication may be reproduced, stored in a retrieval system or transmitted in any way or by any means, electronic, mechanical, photocopying, recording or otherwise, without the prior written permission of the publisher or author.

Cataloguing-in-Publication Data
National Library of Australia
Title: Ignite Your Spark – How To Find Purpose And Take Bold Action Towards Your Dreams
Edition: 1st edn
ISBN: 978-1-9254521-8-1
Category: Self-help/Personal Improvement

The views and opinions expressed in this book are those of the author and do not necessarily reflect the official policy or position of any other agency, publisher, organization, employer or company. Assumptions made in the analysis are not reflective of the position of any entity other than the author(s) — and, these views are always subject to change, revision, and rethinking at any time.

In order to maintain anonymity of certain individuals in some instances names, occupations and places have been changed to protect individuals.

The author, publisher or organizations are not to be held responsible for misuse, reuse, recycled and cited and/or uncited copies of content within this book by others.

*To Igniting Your Spark
And Realising Your Potential*

Love Rebeccah x

DEDICATION

This book is dedicated to you, the reader. For your courage, your curiosity, your passion, enthusiasm for life, your innate knowing that you were born to do something incredible and for your persistence to overcome obstacles, challenges and your fears.

I dedicate this book to your boldest visions, crazy ideas that may one day change the world and your spark that is yet to be ignited bright into the world.

LETTER TO GRANT CARDONE

Grant Cardone,

I don't think I will ever forget your name that's for sure.

A few weeks ago, I took a chance on you. I invested in your Business Bootcamp in Sydney with no idea of what would come of it. Of everything you talked about, the concept of 10Xing was my favourite, but I hadn't taken 10X action in a while. I had been "trying" to write a book, "trying" to grow my business, "trying" to get out there in the world and share my message for years.

At the end of day one, you set my partner Adrian and I a challenge to finish both our books in 5 days. I was terrified I didn't think I would do it, you didn't either. Truth be told, I was hiding behind perfection. And that perfection was keeping me small. Although I made a decision then and there that I wasn't going to play small anymore. As a result of that. You're holding the book in your hands now, we did it!

But Grant, your challenge taught both Adrian and I the most important thing of all. To fail forward, to take imperfect action and believe that it's possible.

I hope you can take a chance on us now and read what we have to share.

Keep 10Xing and we hope to see you again soon.

Kind Regards,

Rebeccah Statham

CONTENTS

Introduction	xii
Part One: Your Bold Vision	1
Your Spark	3
Your Kilimanjaro Awaits	17
What Is A Why?	25
Your Zone Of Genius	37
Redefining Success	43
Stories Of The Possible	49
What's At Stake	55
Part Two: New Beginnings	57
The Magic Of New Beginnings	59
Courage	65
Our Emotions Are Just An Experience	75
Stories	79
Re-write And Redefine	85
What's Your Glass Ceiling?	91
Break That Ceiling!	95
Your Golden Truth	99

Part Three: Brave Action   103

   El Camino De Santiago   105

   ACTion   113

   Who Are You Going To Be?   117

   Your Relationship With Money   121

   Setting Yourself Up For Success   125

   Choosing Your Hard   137

   Be Unapologetic   145

   Power Of Ideas   147

   Get In The Arena. Be Brave And Just Do It.   151

Ignite Your Spark: Interviews With Rebeccah   157

Thank You   161

INTRODUCTION

What is it you deeply want to achieve in your life? What are your unique strengths, passions and grandiose dreams?

What would your life look like if you were igniting your fullest potential?

Scientists estimate that the probability of you being born was a 1 in 400 trillion chance. It's a miracle that you were born here on Earth. To put that into perspective, it's like winning every single lottery — ever!

So, what do you want to do with your miraculous life?

I believe that when you were born into the world, a spark was placed inside of you with one very clear message, to turn it on and shine it bright. Some of you may have no idea that this spark even exists until this very moment. You didn't learn about it at school and there's no traditional science that backs it up. This spark is invisible and isn't located in one particular area of your body. It's ever-present and if you listen to your body, it whispers and gives you messages — you will sense this inner spark.

The more you listen to that flickering spark, the brighter it will shine and the more alive you will feel. The more you remain aware of what you need to feel good and ignite your potential, the more the flame rises.

Your Spark is the goosebumps you feel, that "gut feeling" you cannot explain, the excitement around an idea or a vision you have. It's the subtle voice that whispers to you and nudges you forward — it speaks internally: it may say things like: *you should travel, start a business, quit your job, end that relationship or change careers.*

Your Spark always has the answer and it's been with you since the day you were born. Your Spark holds no judgement towards you, it doesn't care if you have neglected or tried to switch it off. Your Spark is the most loving and forgiving force within you. It knows you, it knows what you're capable of. And whenever you're ready to listen to its inner call, its gentle whispering and the guidance it has for you, it will reveal everything you need to know in order to ignite the light within you.

This book was written for you to *Ignite Your Spark*. It acts as a reminder of your own magnificence and the untapped potential waiting patiently inside of you. It's your reminder that inside of you there is something incredibly powerful to share with the world.

Your Spark has always been there waiting patiently for you to grow its flame to great heights. And when you *Ignite Your Spark*, you'll find yourself living a courageous, bold and unapologetic life of purpose every single day. When you ignite your spark, there's no time to play small, there's only time to be bold and go after the life you desire. Anything and everything is possible, and that's why your spark needs to be ignited and continually fuelled.

We were all born with a spark. You have one, and it's been waiting patiently for you this whole time. You may have experienced moments of it being alight, feeling as if you are undeniably on the right path, that you can do anything in the world. That is what it feels to *Ignite Your Spark*.

Your Spark represents your boldest dreams, visions and goals. It flickers on and off and it is your mission to keep the spark ignited and burning so you can, once and for all, live the life you were born to live.

Before we get started. I want to begin with a story of a golden Buddha. It doesn't matter if this is the first time you've heard it, or the hundredth, there is always a message for you if you're open to it.

Back in 1957, a group of monks from a Buddhist monastery had to relocate a clay Buddha statue from their temple to a new location. As the relocation commenced, the crane lifted the Buddha but it was so heavy that it began to crack, rain began to fall and the head monk was concerned about the potential damage of this sacred Buddha, so they covered it up with a large canvas tarpaulin.

Later that evening, the head monk went to check on the Buddha. As he lifted up the tarp he shone his flashlight and noticed a little gleam shining back at him. He wondered if there was something underneath the clay so he went to fetch his chisel and hammer and began to chip away at the clay. As he knocked off shards of clay, the gleam grew brighter and larger. Hours later, the monk stood back and underneath the clay he discovered a solid-gold Buddha staring back at him.

It was said that hundreds of years ago, monks covered the Buddha to protect it during an invasion but no one lived to tell the tale. The lesson here is that we are all golden Buddhas inside. We were all born with a unique potential to share with the world, and our own quintessential spark lays inside of us. As we have grown, we have piled on our own version of clay in the form of limiting beliefs, fears, stories that prevent us from living an extraordinary life. But with strong vision, courage and unapologetic action we can peel off the layers, just like the monk did, and connect back to our truth.

All over the world, people are seeking meaning in their lives. In fact, if you google, "Find my Purpose," over two-million results come up. But purpose is not "out there" in the world for us to find. It lies deep within us and is our pathway to igniting our spark.

I will never proclaim to be your coach, I am not a psychologist and did not even finish my university degree. But I will be your cheerleader, I will share my stories with you and ask you powerful questions to uncover what really matters to you. I will always believe in you no matter what and I will walk this journey beside you, because I know that together we can do anything.

Lastly, I want to give you permission. Permission to dream big, to be bold and brave. I give you permission to take imperfect action, to ignite your spark, to realise your full potential and to be courageous in pursuit of what sets your heart on fire. I give you permission to fail, to make mistakes, to be vulnerable, to ask for help and to not know all the answers— but to keep going regardless. And lastly, I give you permission to shine your light bright and share your magic with the world.

You've spent your life waiting for permission, so there it is. You have it.

Now, go out there and do something big.

Love Rebeccah x

Part 1:

Your Bold Vision

"You have an inner light within you that is craving to be shared by those around you, by the world at large – but mostly by you. When you share your unique light, bit by bit, you light up the lives of those around you. And, one by one, you inspire them to light up too. It's a chain reaction. And before long, the whole world lights up."
Rebecca Campbell

YOUR SPARK

"The universe buries strange jewels deep within us all, and then stands back to see if we can find them. The hunt to uncover those jewels—that's creative living. The courage to go on that hunt in the first place—that's what separates a mundane existence from a more enchanted one"
Elizabeth Gilbert, Big Magic

Your Spark is the magic inside of you, it's who you are deep within, it's what you stand for and what gifts you want to share with the world. You may be wondering if you have a spark. You absolutely do, it has always been there inside of you.

The journey to reigniting your spark and realising your full potential starts right here. It begins with imagining what's possible for your life. But in order to do that we have to go back to a time when anything was possible, to slowly peel away the clay we have built on top of ourselves.

When I was five years old I belonged to a fairy club and

my fairy name was Starbright. Every few weekends I would join my fellow fairy friends and we would play, dance, eat fairy bread and embrace all the magic there was to experience. Anything and everything was possible when I was Starbright, she believed in magic and truly believed in her heart that anything was possible. As I grew older, fairies became less cool and I was laughed at when people knew that I still believed in them. So I kept Starbright to myself, I dulled down my spark and my magic, although the light dimmed, deep down she's always been there inside of me.

Eventually I stopped believing altogether, I got caught up in trying to be cool and followed the crowd of what everyone else was doing, being popular, liked, admired and valued by those around me. I stopped believing in miracles and possibilities and my dreams, curiosity and belief started to fade. Throughout my teenage years I desperately tried to be liked, to fit in with those around me and to look a certain way.

Looking back, those were some of my saddest moments, I spent years trying to impress everyone around me, I had no idea how to love myself. I was overweight from drinking and eating too much, I wouldn't leave the house without layers of make-up piled on my face. I spent all my hard-earned money on fake Christian Louboutins and the coolest clothes for my nights out and parties. Everything about my life was fake. I had fake friendships, fake IDs for my countless nights out partying on VIP tables, yachts, after-parties, fake tan, fake hair extensions, fake everything. I shut down any relationship or potential partner that tried to get too close to me because I was afraid they would see through the perfected facade I had built around myself. I was covered in layers of clay. The truth was, I was lost and numb. What I learnt is that sometimes we need to lose who we are, in order to find ourselves again. It's taken me years and years to peel off the clay, layer by layer and connect back to my spark. I am so deeply grateful that I chose this life, this incredible life of showing up as *me*. The real me.

I want to tell you now that no matter where you are in your life, no matter how old or how young you are, no matter if you have lived your life igniting your potential or whether you have no idea of where you would even start. It is never too late for you. I am proof of that.

Your Spark is there, it exists. And although I haven't joined up to a fairy club again, I've relearnt that magic still exists. Not in a hocus-pocus sort of way, but I do truly believe that we are on Earth for a reason and anything is possible if we believe it.

I believe you were put here on Earth to not just exist but to live your own path, dream big, and live a life that truly excites you.

Most of us have experienced a time when we stopped dreaming of what was possible.

When was it for you?

It may have been when you got teased for believing in magic? When you got told to "grow up"? When everything suddenly got serious and you were told to be "realistic"?

When suddenly it was time to stop playing and start working and studying?

Think back to the moment when you stopped believing that anything was possible. Do you remember it?

....
....
....

....

....

What did you stop believing?

....

....

....

....

Growing up, most of us thought anything was possible. But as we grew older we were assigned beliefs from our parents, environments and society about who we were – and we listened to them.

Some of us grew up with hard-working parents who believed that the only way to succeed was to get a 9-5 job and work hard until retirement. Some of us grew up with little money or believed that money was bad and every cent should be saved. Some of us were told who we should love and marry, what foods we should eat, what career we should choose, what degree we should study. It's no wonder we have untapped potential lying dormant within us.

School taught us how to memorise ideas and facts and how well we memorised that content would determine if we passed or failed. If we were a good student and passed exams we were rewarded and told we were good enough to keep going. And if we failed, we would often be dropped to either a lower class or our parents were asked why we weren't studying enough.

School wasn't all bad but what it failed to do is recognise our unique gifts, talents and personalities. What it failed to do is teach us how to dream, how to believe in ourselves, how to measure true success, how to discover what excites us and how to realise our full potential.

So now it's up to us to relearn what's possible together. What matters to us. What impact do we want to have on the world. What excites us.

What would you do if anything you imagined was possible?
Think about it for a few minutes.

Would you start building that business you thought of years ago?
Change careers?
Travel the world?
Start studying again?
Move countries?
Redesign your life?

One of my first bold visions was this crazy idea to start a fashion label with no fashion or entrepreneurship experience. After working hard to get great grades and getting into the University of Queensland, I moved halfway across the world from Spain to Brisbane, Australia to start my new life. I was excited to begin a new adventure. Moving across the world to a new country, leaving behind my family, friends and coming to a place where I knew no one was daunting, but I knew it was the right decision.

But something nagged at me. Something about this whole grown-up life didn't sit quite right. All I had learnt from society was to get a degree, a stable job, settle down, save to buy a house, travel once a year and then eventually have kids and settle.

Thank goodness for my parents, because of them I didn't know how to settle. I definitely didn't grow up normal. By the age of three, my parents moved to England and I travelled alongside my dad throughout Europe as he drove trucks. We travelled so much because my mum was a teacher and my dad worked for Caterpillar, and they wanted my 2 sisters and I to see and explore the world.

The only normal period I experienced was from ages four to twelve, where we lived in a small country town in southern New Zealand called Leeston. After moving to Spain at age 12 and then Dubai at age 16, then Argentina by myself and back to Spain briefly before moving to Australia, all I knew was a life of change and adventure.

A year into my university degree, I knew something wasn't right. I knew there was something bigger for my life, I didn't know exactly what it was, but I knew there was something. And all I knew was that I had to trust it; whatever "it" was.

One day, I was trying to find a dress online and ended up scrolling through Alibaba's website (I was most definitely procrastinating during one of my university assignments). Alibaba is the world's biggest online commerce company and it was there that I found all these amazing factories that designed clothing. A bold thought jumped into my mind, *I could start a fashion label.*

Energy whirled up inside of me. Yes, I could create an amazing fashion collection where women would be empowered to feel beautiful and strong. I'd struggled to find a label that resonated with me, one that made me feel empowered. I decided I wanted to design a fashion label that was timeless, luxurious, stunningly simple and allowed the modern-day woman to feel fierce and strong. I would call it Allure Collections. Armed with my new vision, I did something very naïve and perhaps a little crazy, but something that truly excited me.

I dropped out of the business degree I was studying. Saved up all my hard-earned money. Booked a flight to China and before I knew it, I was in the business capital of China, Guangzhou; China's third largest city and home to over 12-million people. English was very scarce and its eclectic blend of modern and ancient worlds somehow weaved themselves into one unique and bustling city.

I spent days and days trolling through markets, wondering what the hell I was doing but burning with excitement at the same time. I remember thinking to myself, *this is what it feels like to truly live*. To be in the unknown, to not know what may happen but to know that anything could happen. Allure Collections was born from that trip and a vision to empower the modern-day woman to feel beautiful, strong and to go after what she wants in life, was born. I saw myself in that vision and wanted to recreate it for others.

Before I knew it, I was running a business at 19 years old. I had photoshoots booked most weekends and was featured in Secrets global jewellery campaign (secrets-shhh.com), I even had one of my designs featured in Richard Branson's very own *Voyeur Magazine* by Virgin.

Now, this fashion label didn't necessarily make thousands and millions of dollars. In fact, it no longer exists. But that's not the point. It was who I became in the process of having a vision that changed my life forever. I became a woman who could go after what she wanted and bring a vision into existence. I felt on purpose, not because being a fashion designer was my purpose, it wasn't that at all. I felt on purpose because I connected to a vision that excited me and I was unapologetic in bringing that vision into the world regardless of how much money I earnt from it.

The thing about igniting your spark is that it truly is a journey of the unknown. But having a vision is crucial if you're willing to take the journey of discovery.

So, ask yourself. Where are you going? What are you doing? What do you believe is possible in your life?

Don't just read the words — really think about them.

Why do you get up in the morning? Why do you go to work every day and choose to give someone eight to nine hours of your precious time?

*If you don't know or you feel unfulfilled in what you're currently doing, use this space to reflect on what it is you would love to be doing with your days.

YOUR SPARK

"If you are working on something that you really care about, you don't have to be pushed. The vision pulls you."
Steve Jobs

Keeping the Spark Alive

Sometimes, in order to go forward we need to take a few steps backwards. I invite you to take a step back in time. Think about who you wanted to be when you were younger, when you were around five years old. What were the things you loved?

Think back to the carefree times when you didn't care what you looked like, being judged or having your dreams stifled. When you did not care about much, apart from eating and sleeping and playing; before all the rules, roles and social conditioning came into place.

Who were you? What mattered to you? What did you believe in? When you can ask yourself those questions, you can dive deep into the core of who you are and discover what really matters to you.

Big Questions for Big Living

No matter who you are, how old you are, where you are from or what you have believed before this moment, you have the potential to bring forth a magic that has never yet existed in the world.

Ask yourself big questions.

What do I want?

....
....
....
....

What life do I want to live?

....
....

Who do I want to be?

How much money do I want to earn?

What kind of work do I want to be doing?

What kind of relationships do I want?

Do I want to travel?

....
....
....
....

Do I want to start a charity?

....
....
....
....

What do I want to be remembered for?

....
....
....
....

You are someone that has the potential to create massive waves in the world. If you do not see your vision, how can you know what's possible? To create your vision, you have to dream and think bigger, you have to look at what is possible in your life and go after it.

And in the words of Danielle La Porte, "Who were you before the world told you who you were?"

"The way we experience the world around us is a direct reflection of the world within us. If our thoughts and energy are not supportive, then our life won't be supported. Therefore, we must take responsibility by consciously supporting ourselves in every given moment."
Gabrielle Bernstein

YOUR KILIMANJARO AWAITS

"It's not the mountain we conquer but ourselves."
Sir Edmund Hillary

What is a goal that you've had for a while that absolutely scares you?

What challenges have you faced lately? Where have you pushed yourself for growth?

And what is your vision? What is it that you dream of achieving in your life?

No matter where you are along your journey, we all have a mountain to climb. Some of you may be climbing with a strong vision straight to the top, whilst others are taking the scenic route and wandering along stopping along the way. Some of you may be at the beginning of your mountain, whilst others are in the rocky terrain climbing. I don't know where you are right now – but wherever you are, I want you to know that whatever is at the top of your mountain, you have the power to get there.

To realise our full potential, we must face and conquer our own mountains.

Just so we are clear, there are no hacks to the top. You will face challenges that push you to your limits and you'll discover that comfort is very scarce on the journey. But what I can assure you is that you will grow and transform; and what lies on the other side of the climb is the most astounding beauty you have ever seen. The mountain represents the challenge, your goal and vision. But the mountain I'm about to share with you is one I climbed in 2013 when I was 17. Its name is Mt Kilimanjaro and it is the tallest free-standing mountain in the world.

I lived in Dubai at the time and a former teacher from my school had been taking people up the mountain for a few years. It was my final year of school and I knew this was my last opportunity to go before I left Dubai. I liked the idea of climbing a mountain and I had always wanted to go to Africa, plus every week a group of us trained together, and I got to hang out with some girls from school which was fun, so that was a great bonus. As the deadline got closer and closer to leaving I made sure I had all the right gear, I had my torch, snacks, boots, sleeping bags and all the right clothes. I even had a special CamelBak waterbag with a special protective layer so my water didn't freeze in cold temperatures. I was set to begin my journey climbing. Or so I thought.

What I had extremely underestimated was the physical training required to climb this mountain. Mt Kilimanjaro is also known as the roof of Africa, because it is the highest point of Africa. With most things in my life, preparation wasn't my strength and I had left my physical training to the absolute last minute. As I read more and more about the climb, I started to panic. I remember my dad making me run around the block with a snorkel in my mouth to prepare me for the lack of oxygen I would endure whilst climbing. He would also make me run on the beach up and down in the middle of an Arabian summer which was around 45 degrees Celsius to get my fitness up. But no amount of last-minute trainings could really make up for my lack of preparation and before I knew it I was on the plane to Tanzania.

As I flew into Tanzania I caught a glimpse of the magnificent mountain I was about to climb. It was huge. And I remember thinking 'Wow, I can't believe I'm going to do this.' I was both scared and excited but I knew I had come too far to not make it. Something inside of me was determined to make it no matter what. I was the least fit out of my group, so I vowed that I would run my own race. I would walk at my own pace and no matter what it took, I would get to the top.

Day one approached and we arrived at our starting point. We had seven days in total, six days up and one day down. We had decided to take the longer route in order to acclimatise as much as possible. This involved climbing up and climbing down the mountain to get used to the lack of oxygen that the 5,895 metres above sea level mountain presented. Twenty minutes into the climb I was out of breath! *Already*, I thought.

We were trekking through rainforest and up an incredible steep hill. By the end of the day I was far behind the group and I was exhausted. Hindsight is a great thing, and I envied everyone else who was fitter and stronger than me. But I knew it was my own doing and so all I could do was control one foot in front of the other. What kept me going was our porters that were with us on our journey. They were local Tanzanian people who helped carry our tents and food supplies and always with the biggest smile on their faces. They would repeat a Swahili phrase to us *Poli Poli. Poli Poli* which meant slowly, slowly.

Altitude sickness can be fatal, so taking it slow was the key to surviving and conquering the climb. I don't think I had a choice but to take the local's advice as everyone sped ahead. My dad had also packed me little notes to open each day, they were the best comfort and the only comfort I had during that trip. Every morning I looked forward to opening them. They would say things like, "I'm so proud of you, keep going." In the times where I wanted to give up, I would reread those messages and keep repeating them to myself.

As the days went by, we climbed and climbed. We climbed through the rainforest and into the rocky terrain eventually climbing through the clouds and up and up the mountain.

Each night I would go to bed, my muscles screaming, exhausted from the day of intensive climbing. I wanted to cry and give up so many times and sometimes I did cry and wish that I could go home. But I knew I had to push through, I had to keep going.

Some nights we would be sleeping on rocks and the higher we climbed the less oxygen we had so breathing became more and more difficult. Throughout the seven-day hike there were no showers or toilets that were in condition worth using. We would use baby wipes to "shower" off the dirt and sweat and ducking in the bush became a regular activity.

As I mentioned, comfort is not something that is present on the journey. Day four into the climb, the sun was out, although it didn't feel warm when we were walking up the mountain, I made the mistake of not putting on sunscreen and due to the close proximity to the sun and my fair complexion, that night when we reached camp I noticed these pus-filled lumps all over my arms, scalp and neck.

I was so sunburnt that I had hundreds of blisters filled with puss all over my arms and in my hair. It was excruciating and I barely slept from the pain. Not to mention extremely gross too! There were no doctors and so I had to lather on whatever was in our First-aid kit and cover my arms. On top of that, the same night, I got my period. This was almost my breaking point. That night I left my tent in the freezing cold, took my headlight and climbed up the rocky ridge to try get some reception. When I finally got a bar of signal, I called my parents and thank goodness, they picked up. I can't remember what they said or what I said but all I knew was I couldn't turn back. I was so close and had already come so far and to turn back now would mean to give up. The mountain had broken me physically, but it could not break me mentally. All I had was my mind, the thoughts I could control and the will to slowly keep walking.

    I kept repeating the Swahili phrase in my head, *"poli poli Bec. You can do this. Keep walking and keep going."* Eventually, I made it to summit night.

    Summit night was something else. We packed up our stuff and left our tent at around 9 pm in the freezing cold and we started the 10-hour climb to Uhuru Peak. It was dark and with our headlights you could only focus on the person in front of you, putting one foot in front of the other. One hour into the climb my super-gadget CamelBak that had its extra protection so that the water wouldn't freeze, froze. It was classic. So, I knew for the next fifteen or so hours, the time it would take to get up to the summit and back down, there would be no water. The cold made it almost impossible but you couldn't stop. The risk of hypothermia was real and if I had stopped physically I don't know if my body could have started again. As we climbed up and up the oxygen got thinner and thinner. We had to take huge breaths in and barely any oxygen filled our lungs, it was exhausting. Around five hours into the climb people started turning back, altitude sickness started to hit and people around me started vomiting and had to stop due to excruciating headaches. Some people couldn't make it and had to start ascending as extreme altitude sickness can be fatal. We had porters around us supporting us and at one stage the altitude hit me gently. I became dizzy and my vision went slightly blurry. A porter grabbed me and guided me until I felt able again to keep going.

Slowly, slowly the hours passed and I kept putting one foot in front of the other. I kept repeating over and over, "Bec you can do this", "you are so strong", "you are capable of doing this", "you can do it". I didn't stop. Eventually, the sun started to rise upon the glaciers. When other people stopped to rest, I kept walking because at this point I had nothing left inside of me but the will to keep going forward. I thought of my dad and mum who were so proud of me and how proud of myself I was for pushing through. I kept walking, past the ice glaciers and around the ridge of the mountain to reach the peak. I had spent the climb at the back, not running anyone else's race but my own. The people who had been rushing up the mountain got hit badly with altitude sickness and were unable to finish. One foot in front of the other, with my incredible porter beside me I was the first female and the second person in our group of fifteen to reach the peak. I stood on the roof of Africa holding my New Zealand flag at the top. I had done it. I had climbed the mountain. It was the most magnificent view I have ever seen and in that moment, everything was worth it.

What is the mountain you need to climb?

....

....

....

....

How can *Poli Poli* help you in your climb?

....

....

....

....

There are so many lessons to take out of this story, the biggest one being that no matter who you are or your current ability or strengths you can truly do anything you put your mind to. Yes, preparation helps and in hindsight I would have trained more. But how often do we over-prepare, over-think, over-question, over-analyse every single move that we make?

How often do we let the fear or challenge of our mountain prevent us from taking any action? When all we need to do is take the very first step.

Our visions, our dreams and our biggest goals are our own internal GPS system that is built into us. It will always find a way to get there. You make take the scenic route, the route to acclimatise which means you may go up and down a few times. Or you may take the direct route and have to stop and rest before you burn out. Whichever way you take, don't think too much. Just take one step forward and *poli poli*.

Let's begin climbing.

"You're off to Great Places!
Today is your day!
Your mountain is waiting,
So... get on your way!"
Dr. Seuss,
Oh, The Places You'll Go!

+++

Rebeccah on the summit of Kilimanjaro.

WHAT IS A WHY?

Let's get one thing clear, your purpose and your why are basically the same thing, it really doesn't matter which word you use. What matters is that you understand what it means to you. In France they call it *raison d'être*, in Japan they call it *Ikagai*, which translates to *reason for being*.

Your WHY is your own interpretation, it's what matters most to you, whether you know it yet or not. We all have a *reason for being* deep inside. It can be as simple or as complex as you like. Sometimes we make finding our WHY and our purpose complicated, we assume it has to be this big thing and needs to change the world. When in fact, all it has to change is our own world, and by changing our world, maybe one day, that will change the world.

Steve Jobs said, "You can't connect the dots looking forward; you can only connect them looking backwards. So you have to trust that the dots will somehow connect in your future." And when I looked back to connect the dots of all the things I loved, my WHY was staring right back at me. I looked at the books I read, the conversations I had in cafes with complete strangers, the businesses I connected with, the workshops I attended, the jobs I loved and equally the jobs that sucked the life out of me. It was all so clear.

My why was to Ignite Spark in people's lives so that they could realise their full potential and empower others to do the same.

I was always searching for purpose in my life, but when I connected to my why I realised that, whatever I did from this moment on as long as I connected to my WHY, I would always feel on purpose.

The most inspiring people in the world aren't going out there and trying to inspire. They are doing what they love every single day and they're connected to a WHY that's driving and pushing them forward.

One of my favourite stories is from President John F. Kennedy who visited the NASA Space Center back in 1962. He noticed a janitor carrying a broom and he walked over to the janitor and said, "Hi, I'm Jack Kennedy. What are you doing?"

"Well, Mr. President," the janitor responded, "I'm helping put a man on the moon."

To most people, this janitor was just cleaning the building. But his contribution was connected to something so much larger. He was a part of making history. That is the impact when you connect to your WHY. No matter what you do or how you do it, when you connect to your WHY, your *ikigai*, your *raison d'être*... whatever you name it, every day will feel on purpose.

The most important thing about a WHY is that it gives you focus and direction. It is your body's own internal GPS system that guides the way in times of uncertainty, hardship, failure and tough times. When you plug in your WHY and connect to it daily throughout your life you will find yourself igniting your spark and living your dream life, one that is in alignment with what truly matters to you. You may meander, take short-cuts or take the scenic route, you may even end up at an unexpected but better destination or take time to stop for a while. Your journey however, is yours. You get to design and recreate it, and anything is possible when you start focusing on what it is that you truly love and want for your life.

Finding Your Why

So, how do you go about finding your WHY when you have absolutely no idea where to look?

Curiosity is a great way to begin and is the one thing that will always point you in the right direction.

What are you curious about trying? What excites you? Where do you love spending your time? What are the common themes in your life? Where do your strengths lie? What corner of the bookstore could I find you in? What do you watch on YouTube? What are you interests? Which parts of your work do you love? What parts don't you love? When did you last feel extremely proud of yourself? What are some of the peak moments in your life that have truly shaped who you are?

It's very easy to be overwhelmed with all of these questions, so take some time to reflect and get curious. Below is some space for you to journal and ponder.

Write your thoughts down, write words that feel good to you and remember that you can't get this wrong.

IGNITE YOUR SPARK

In my life, what am I willing to stand for?

....

....

....

....

Hopefully by now you should have an idea of what matters to you, which in its essence is your WHY. The powerful thing about having a WHY is that it's yours and nobody can take it away from you. As you grow and adapt, your WHY may also shift. Remember that you are not meant to stay the same, as you grow and take action towards your dreams and goals you will transform in ways you can't even imagine. So, if one day you wake up and your WHY has shifted, then go and explore that. Always be curious and never stop believing in your ability to change your life. It all begins here, this whole chapter has been dedicated to creating your vision because it is the internal GPS, the building blocks of everything else that is it to come.

Creating Your Why Statement
A powerful way to encapsulate your WHY is to create a WHY Statement. This is an extremely effective way to communicate your why to others. Your WHY Statement should be simple, clear and written in affirmative language that resonates with you. Your Statement will be the guiding light that will be used as your GPS destination so where possible it would be applicable to both your work and personal life and not mutually exclusive. In the book, *Find Your Why*, Simon Sinek explained that your WHY Statement is "a statement of your value at work as much as it is the reason your friends love you. We don't have a professional WHY

and personal WHY. We are who we are wherever we are. Your contribution is not a product or a service. It's the thing around which everything you do — the decisions you make, the tasks you perform, the products you sell — aligns to bring about the impact you envision."

The Formula

Simon Sinek devised the WHY formula to inspire everyone to clearly express their unique contribution and impact on the world. He believes that everyone has a WHY and when you can put words to your WHY, you gain clarity and direction to find the work, relationships and organisations in which you feel most fulfilled.

<u>YOUR WHY STATEMENT FORMULA</u>

TO _____ SO THAT _____ .

The first blank represents your *contribution* — the contribution you make to the lives of others through your WHY. And the second blank represents the *impact* of your contribution.

Your job is to plug-in the blanks to create your own unique WHY Statement.

Before you create your own, here are some examples of other people and companies' statements.

> **1. Simon Sinek's WHY Statement:**
> To inspire people to do the things that inspire them so that, together we can change our world.
> https://simonsinek.com
>
> **2. Brainy Box's WHY Statement:**
> We exist to 'Spark life' in the workplace, so that people can feel their best and be their best where they spend

most of their time.
https://brainybox.com.au

3. Airbnb's WHY Statement:
To connect millions of people in real life all over the world, through a community marketplace – so that you can Belong Anywhere.
https://www.airbnb.com.au/

4. Momenton's WHY Statement:
To empower the modern enterprise through technology so that, together we can challenge the norm and enable impactful change.
https://momenton.com.au

5. Rebeccah Statham's WHY Statement:
To Ignite Spark in people's lives, so that they can realise their full potential and empower others to do the same.
https://www.igniteandco.com
https://www.rebeccahstatham.com

Remember that your WHY statement needs to capture the contribution and impact that excites you the most. Now it's your turn.

You can create an individual WHY, or use it to create a WHY for your business. As long as it is aligned to the life you want to stand for, that's all that matters.

TO ....

SO THAT ....

Golden Circle

Now you have your WHY, what's next?

Well, as you can tell I'm a little Simon Sinek obsessed because I'm going to share with you another one of his tools called the Golden Circle. Sinek built this circle based on three elements.

1. **What** we do
2. **How** we do it
3. **Why** we do it

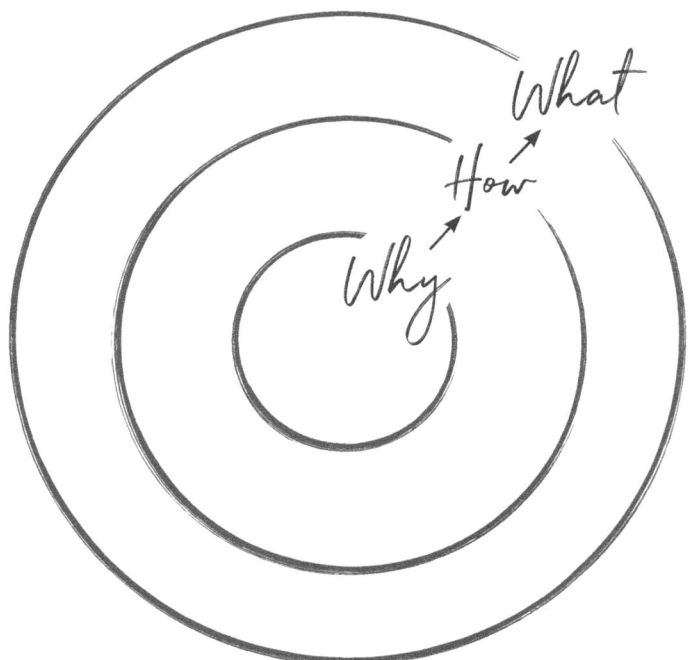

Before we begin to dive into this, you are already ahead of the game. Why? Because you have your WHY statement. Simon built this circle to show that most people operate from the outside-in. They know what they do (let's use an accountant for example), they know how they do it (analysing data, finance reports, budgets, tax returns, and accounting records) but when asked WHY most of them would have no idea.

They may say something like, "It's what I have always done" or "It's what I studied at university" or "It was the highest paying job I could get to pay off my mortgage", "It's what I'm good at"... etc.

Now, people who are connected to a WHY may have a completely different answer but I'm talking generally about most people in today's society. According to a 2017 study in *The State of the Global Workplace* report from Gallup[1], only 14% of employees in Australia and New Zealand are engaged in their jobs. That means statistically 86% of employees in Australia and New Zealand are not engaged in what they do. But there is a way to change that, and you can be a part of the change simply by using the Golden Circle because when you can align to your why everything shifts.

Remember back to the story of the janitor whose why was to send people to the moon? Well now it's time for you to create your own story.

---

1. Gallup, 2017, *State of the Global Workplace, Executive Summary*, Washington, www.gallup.com

MY WHY:

TO _____

SO THAT _____

↓

HOW I DO THAT:

....

....

....

↓

WHAT I DO:

....

....

....

Play around with these examples. Your how and what will change all the time depending on what you do. But your core WHY should stay the same for the time being. Also, remember that making money is a result of what you do when you connect to your WHY and shouldn't be used as your core WHY.

I also invite you to start talking to your WHY. Start living and breathing it now.

Job crafting is an incredible way to start doing this and is a great way to craft your role to enable you to do more of what you love. 'Job crafting' is all about reimagining your current career or job. This term was coined and researched by Amy Wrzesniewski, professor of organisational behaviour at the Yale School of Management. She describes it as being able to "reshape and reimagine how you can make your current role work for you, inspire, and excite you."

Let's face it, there's always going to be parts of your role that you don't particularly enjoy but if you can identify areas that you love and align them with your WHY you'll find yourself much more engaged in what you do.

+++

"Reach out, share your truth, tell someone, "This is who I am. This is what I stand for. Hold me to it." Often, we'll do far more for another than we will do for ourselves."
Kamal Ravikant, Live Your Truth

+++

The next time someone asks, "What do you do?", I challenge you to say your WHY Statement. Because that is who you are and what you represent.

From this moment on you will never let your role title or what you do define who you are. From this moment, who you are is who you decide to be and what you choose to stand for.

German philosopher, Frederick Nietzsche once said, "He who has a why can endure any how." Having a strong WHY is like the energy of light focused through a magnifying glass. Diffused light has little use, but when concentrated through a magnifying glass that same light can set fire to paper. Concentrated even more, that light can cut steel. If you think about it, there is nothing that separates you and I from anyone else in the world. All it comes down to is what are you willing to stand for, who are you willing to be and what impact do you want to have on the world?

When you get clear on that, nothing can stand in your way.

+++

"Each experience in your life was absolutely necessary in order to have gotten you to the next place, and the next place, up to this very moment."
Dr. Wayne Dyer

YOUR ZONE OF GENIUS

Now that you've defined your WHY Statement, let's discover your Zone of Genius. You might be wondering what a zone of genius is and if you have one. Dr. Wayne Dyer, known as the father of motivation said that "Genius is a potential that lives within you and every other human being. You have many moments of genius in your lifetime. These are the times when you have a uniquely brilliant idea and implement it even if only you are aware of how fantastic it is."

So yes, we all have a genius within us and you'll find that's where the magic happens. Our Zone of Genius is our super power. Often times it lies at the intersection of our innate talents and passions, and is often difficult to distinguish because it comes so naturally to us. Because we are engineered and built so uniquely, no one can ever replicate your Zone of Genius, it belongs to you and when you ignite your spark and realise your full potential, you will find yourself sharing your genius with the world.

Getting in the zone

In his book, *The Big Leap*, Gay Hendricks identified four different zones that we spend our time in, with only one of them being our Zone of Genius. They are listed below and I invite you to look at where you are spending most of your time and energy.

1. The Zone of Incompetence – These are all the activities we're not good at. Others can do them a lot better than we can although surprisingly we spend a lot of time here trying to figure it out!

As a new entrepreneur, it's very easy to spend a lot of time in the Zone of Incompetence. Because you have to do everything yourself. What started as an exciting idea and bold vision means you're now spending your time and energy-learning accounting, building websites, social media platforms, SEO, CRM systems... and trying to figure it all out whilst building the business. If we're not careful and spend too much time in The Zone of Incompetence we can become frustrated, dejected and give up.

Where are you currently spending time in your Zone of Incompetence?

....

....

....

If you have the money, can you hire someone to help you? Or is there someone you can ask for help?

....

....

On that note, do you struggle to ask for help? If so, how can you get better at it?

2. The Zone of Competence – You're competent at the activities in the Zone of Competence, but others can do them just as well. Successful people often discover that they spend far too much time and energy in this zone.

How much time are you wasting doing menial tasks? Are your prioritising cleaning your house? Cooking every single meal? Washing and ironing every few days? Doing all the food shopping?

Don't get me wrong, these things all need to be done. But are you spending too much time in this zone when you could delegate these tasks?

When writing this book for example, I noticed I was spending a lot of my time and energy cooking. I only had small pockets of time to write as I still work full time so I decided to delegate that and buy pre-made healthy meals to save time and energy.

At the end of the day, you need to find what works best for you, but be careful of the trap. It's a great way of procrastinating!

Where are you currently spending time in your Zone of Competence?

....
....
....
....

Where can you delegate some of these tasks to free up time for you to be in your Zone of Genius?

....
....
....
....

3. The Zone of Excellence – In the Zone of Excellence are the activities you do extremely well. You make a good living in your Zone of Excellence, which makes it a seductive and dangerous trap as it is so easy to stay here. The temptation is strong to remain in the Zone of Excellence; it's where your own addiction to comfort wants you to stay. It's also where your family, friends, and organisation wants you to stay.

What is your Zone of Excellence?

....
....
....
....

Where have you been spending time in your Zone of Excellence?

....

....

....

....

4. The Zone of Genius – Hendricks outlines that The Zone of Genius is where you find your "flow", the activities where time simply disappears, the place where you tap into your creativity and express your natural genius (which are your innate skills and unique strengths). Liberating and expressing your natural genius is your ultimate path to success and life satisfaction. Your Zone of Genius is the set of activities you are uniquely suited to that enable you to draw on your special gifts and strengths.

When I think of people in their zone of genius, I think of Steve Jobs who paved the vision for Apple, Elon Musk envisioning a new future of SpaceX and Tesla, Richard Branson who founded Virgin Group which controls more than 400 companies, Lisa Messenger who founded The Collective Hub whose WHY is to ignite human potential and be an entrepreneur for entrepreneurs, and lastly Albert Einstein who developed the theory of relativity and famously said "Everybody is a genius. But if you judge a fish by its ability to climb a tree, it will spend its whole life believing that it is stupid."

We all have a genius inside of us. What is yours?

....

....

What are your innate strengths and passions?

If you could spend the rest of your life in your Zone of Genius, what would you be doing?

What are you doing when you lose track of time, feel in your flow and are doing what you love most?

> "The problem is that a deep, sacred part of you will wither and die if you stay inside your Zone of Excellence. There is only one place where you will ultimately thrive and feel satisfied, and that's... The Zone of Genius."
> **Gay Hendricks**

REDEFINING SUCCESS

We all want to experience success, but what does success feel like to you? How have you been measuring it? And have you ever considered that success may not be what you thought it was?

Before we realise our potential and ignite our spark we have to define what success means to us.

Margie Warrell, bestselling author and internationally recognised leader in human potential said that "unless you take the time to decide what it truly means for you to live a successful life you can wind up spending your entire life working desperately hard to never measure up to the definitions that others have created for you."

Society's definition of success often leaves you forever striving and never feeling good enough.

Without knowing who you are, what excites you and what you want to create in your life, you will never feel truly successful. It doesn't matter whether you're earning $20,000/year or $200,000/year – if you don't live your life in alignment with what's intrinsically driving you, no amount of external validation or success will make you happy.

We live in a society where everything external is positioned to make us feel like we need its presence to be happy. We depend on external gratification and are made to believe that by driving a certain car, dating a certain calibre of person, obtaining a certain role in a company, having the best clothes, or by earning a certain amount of money that we are "successful".

Most of society's viewpoints on success are focused on looking a certain way which leaves a lot of people constantly striving for more, pushing for that next promotion, the next pay rise but never truly feeling they're enough. It explains why people who seem to have it all together on the outside are unhappy, depressed and lonely. Jim Carrey said, "I think everybody should get rich and famous and do everything they ever dreamed of so they can see that it's not the answer". Because there is an underlying belief that money, wealth, success and fame will bring us happiness. And that's simply not the case.

The current stats on mental health from Beyond Blue show that 1 million Australian adults have depression and over 2 million have anxiety.[1] Depression and anxiety are now seen as the most common mental health issues and suicide remains the leading cause of death for Australians aged between 15 and 44.

Having experienced anxiety and depression and lost a friend to suicide, I know what it feels like to have no sense of worth. To feel like who I am is not enough. From the outside looking in, I truly did look like I had everything together. In fact, no one would have known if I hadn't of opened up and shared it with people. I had a comfortable six-figure income, was a successful senior consultant at the

---

1. https://www.beyondblue.org.au/the-facts

world's largest recruiting firm, had an incredible loving partner and great friends around me. But I was so dependent on my life looking a certain way and when I got what I had always wanted – I realised that I had been well and truly missing the point.

My work gave me crippling anxiety, I was stressed to the bone and people stopped complimenting me on how "great" I was looking after losing all this weight and started to become concerned that I was becoming too thin. The truth was, I was so anxious and stressed, my body was burning everything I ate at such a fast rate and my adrenal glands were smashed. I was exhausted and had no idea what success was anymore. Why did I feel so empty? What I discovered was that my definition of success was borrowed, I had believed that by obtaining a certain amount of things, I would feel like a success. What I felt instead was depleted, uninspired and empty. So I had to relearn what success was for me. I had to reach this point to learn that what I had believed was not the answer. As Leonard Cohen says, "There is a crack in everything, that's how the light gets in". By breaking down, I was able to let the light shine in and redefine my version of success.

What borrowed beliefs do you currently have around being "successful"?

....

....

....

My hope for you is that you do not reach the breaking point that I, and so many people have. And if you are at breaking point, know that you can and will get through this. Know that sometimes you need to breakdown in order to rebuild and let the light shine through.

There are many definitions of success, but my favourite is one by Earl Nightingale. Nightingale said, "Success is the progressive realization of a worthy goal or ideal. This means that any person who knows what they are doing and where they are going is a success. Any person with a goal towards which they are working is a successful person."

How does this measure up to how you currently define success?

....

....

....

....

Notice that Nightingale doesn't suggest that you become successful once you have obtained something – rather, it's the process of working towards a goal that is the success. Most of us believe that we are only successful after the obtainment of the goal. We say things like "When I have this, then I'll be able to do that", "When I lose ten kilos, then I will wear a bikini on the beach", "When I'm in a safe secure job, then I will start a passion project", "When I have paid off my mortgage then I will finally travel and do all the things I want to do with my life".

Instead of letting your circumstances dictate when you can start taking action towards your goals, ask yourself today "who can I be today, what actions do I need to take in order to have the life of my dreams and get closer to my goals?"

When you start acting from this space, you redefine your definition of success. If who you are being is getting you closer to what you want, then to Nightingale's description you are a success right now. By going to the gym, sitting down and registering your ABN, writing a business plan for your next project — you are a success. Success breeds success, the more you believe in your success, the more it will keep coming to you.

Remember that everyone will have their own version of success, but that does not stop you from creating your own version.

If you had to redefine what success meant for you, what would it be?

....
....
....
....

Who do you need to be today?

....
....
....
....

What actions do you need to take to have your dream life?

....
....
....
....
....
....

"Success and failure come and go, but don't let them define you. It's who you are that matters."
Kamal Ravikant, Live Your Truth

STORIES OF THE POSSIBLE

As humans, our beliefs around what's possible are changing all the time. The more we continue to challenge the norm, the more we form new beliefs that challenge what we once thought was impossible.

In the 19th century, people believed that if steam trains went faster than 50km per hour the human body would explode. Eventually someone was brave enough to challenge that belief and found that bodies did not actually explode. And thank goodness someone was brave enough to challenge that.

Another great example is the four-minute mile that was deemed impossible to break before Roger Banister proved that it could be done. 46 days after, John Landy broke the barrier again. A year later, more and more people broke the barrier in a single race. It wasn't that all of a sudden people became faster runners – rather, an outdated belief was broken and a new norm had been created. Belief led these people to accomplish something that was previously deemed impossible.

Having a strong vision and dreaming big is the fuel that drives us over the bridge from the present and into our future. Without vision, you'll wander around life letting others tell you what to do and where to go. You'll keep living your life the way it has always been. You'll feel tired and unfulfilled because you don't have a clear vision of what you want.

As Zig Ziglar said, "Lack of direction, not lack of time, is the problem. We all have twenty-four hour days."

The question is, what are you going to do with your time? It's never a case of if you're ready, it's a case of when you are ready. Life is what we make of it and it is never too late to start imagining what is possible for our lives.

- What would you do with your life if you knew you could not fail?

....
....
....
....
....

- What would you do with your days If you had all the time and money in the world?

....
....
....
....
....

- And how would you wake up in the morning if you knew that anything was possible?

....
....
....
....
....

Below are some stories of incredible people, who against all odds, believed in the power of their dreams and went on to impact the world.

- Walt Disney was fired from a newspaper job early on because he "lacked imagination". He was turned down by over a hundred banks when he tried to get funding to develop Disneyland and had several bankruptcies before Disneyland was born.

- Colonel Harland Sanders was fired multiple times and forced to retire, he found himself broke and worried about how he was going to survive off his $105 monthly pension cheque. He decided to drive around, sleep in his car and desperately try to find a restaurant that would franchise the secret recipe he had perfected over the years. He was rejected more than 1,000 times before KFC was born.

- Albert Einstein was considered an "unteachable fool" by his early teachers.

- Michael Jordan was cut from his high school basketball team. He quotes "I've failed over and over again in my life, and that is why I succeed."

- Stephen Hawking was known for his groundbreaking ideas on the laws that govern the universe. But when he was 21, Stephen was diagnosed with Motor Neurone Disease. He has never let this disease stop him from following his passion and bringing his ideas to the world.

- In his early teens, Jim Carrey and his family were so poor they lived in a van. So, Jim dropped out of school to support his family. In the 1990s, he was known as a struggling actor just getting by, so to stay motivated he wrote himself a cheque for $10 million dollars for "acting services rendered," dated for 1994. He carried this around for daily inspiration and in 1994, Jim landed the role for *Dumb and Dumber* earning exactly $10 million!

- Oprah was born into poverty to a single mother and was sexually abused on multiple occasions by family members and a close friend. She had all odds against her but told herself that this would not be her life. She is now one of the most influential women in the world and a multi-billionaire.

- After the death of her mother, JK Rowling was recently divorced and considered herself the biggest failure she knew. Living in a cramped apartment with her daughter, jobless and penniless, Rowling fell into a deep depression and admits she even considered suicide. Her first Harry Potter book was rejected 12 times before it was finally accepted. It is now valued at $15 billion.

- Vera Wang started her career as an athlete but failed to qualify for the 1968 Olympic figure skating team. She is now one of the biggest names in fashion today after she started designing wedding dresses at age 40. Her business is now worth over a billion dollars.

Now, how is your story going to sound? Are you going to continue walking around blindly with no clear direction? Or are you going to get clear on your vision and imagine what's possible for your life?

You always have a choice, you just have to reimagine what's possible.

What's Your Story Going to Be?

"When you are inspired by some great purpose, some extraordinary project, all your thoughts break their bonds: Your mind transcends limitations, your consciousness expands in every direction, and you find yourself in a new, great and wonderful world. Dormant forces, faculties and talents become alive, and you discover yourself to be a greater person by far than you ever dreamed yourself to be."
Patanjali

WHAT'S AT STAKE?

We often fail to think of the bigger impact that *not* taking action can have, not only on ourselves but on the people around us.

When you *Ignite Your Spark* you inspire those around you to ignite their spark too. I want you to imagine yourself living your dream life and by doing so all the people you're able to inspire and impact too.

The power of you realising your full potential and sharing that with the world is undeniably one of the greatest things anyone can do in the world. Because what if everything changed? And alternatively, how would you feel if nothing changed?

Dr Wayne Dyer said, "Don't die with the music still inside of you." What he meant was that we all hear a different sound, a melody that plays within us. These are our biggest and wildest dreams, niggling ideas and opportunities that often lie dormant inside just waiting for the chance to be expressed.

Everyone's "music" is different, so don't get caught up comparing or judging if your music sounds unique, it's supposed to. Find the music inside of you, dance to it, have fun with it and don't stop listening to it. Express it until your very last breath.

The one certainty we have in life is that one day our time here will end. We don't know when or how, but what is certain is that someday our time will be up. So, what is it that you want to do here in the world?

I want you to imagine what it would feel like to have your dream life. Imagine how your days flow living life in alignment with your *why*. Imagine all the incredible people you interact with and waking up so excited about the days ahead.

All of this is possible for you.

Most success stories have a deeper story behind them. If you think of any successful person you admire, it started with them having the courage to dance to the music they heard, no matter how unique or crazy it sounded.

Don't let the world *not* see your spark because you're too busy trying to find the perfect way to shine. Go out and imagine what's possible for your life because anything and everything is possible.

Part 2: New Beginnings

"I've learned that fear is simply an illusion based on past experiences that we project into the present and onto the future."
Gabrielle Bernstein

THE MAGIC OF NEW BEGINNINGS

"There is this space between one chapter and the next where nothing makes sense everything is unknown and life is uncomfortable. It is the space that makes most of us want to run and cling onto the next familiar thing. But if you resist and stay in this restless space. If you invite in all your fears and shadows. From this space your brightest dreams begin to bloom. I call this space the dark magic of new beginnings."
Vienda Maria

Take a moment to breathe and acknowledge yourself for a moment. I hope you are proud of how far you've come. I'm not talking about how far you've progressed in the book, but how far you've come in your life. Every journey, every obstacle, every mountain you've had to climb has led you to this very moment. And you are now here, with me igniting the incredible spark that is within you.

To create an extraordinary life comes with a decision

to truly create a change, a commitment to realise what's possible in our lives and a willingness to do whatever it takes to create the opportunities. You have what it takes, now all that's needed is for you to bridge the gap between where you are now and where you want to be. And in order to do that, there are a few things to consider. First of all, what's currently holding you back? Is it fear? Your level of belief? Your worthiness? Your excuses? What is it? Now of course, not every change you create in your life will challenge you! But the big decisions and the big leaps into the unknown will.

Let's start with fear. Fear can play a huge part in our lives if we let it. Fear lies in the gap between where we are now, to where we ultimately want to be. It lies in the disguise of obstacles, imagined stories and limiting beliefs. No matter what, fear will humbly remind us of our existence. That we are alive, that we feel things deeply and that deep down we are all scared of failing. But fear is not something to be afraid of, in fact feeling fear is a great sign that what you're doing matters.

Often, we try to run away from fear when it shows up, scientists describe this as the "fight or flight" response, in which our brains are wired to either fight through a dangerous situation or run from it. Elizabeth Gilbert, author of *Eat Pray Love* and *Big Magic* says that "Your fear is like a mall cop who thinks he's a Navy SEAL: He hasn't slept in days, he's all hopped up on Red Bull, and he's liable to shoot at his own shadow in an absurd effort to keep everyone 'safe'."

Now, don't get me wrong in some cases fear can be extremely useful which is why you will never hear me using the term "fearless". There are moments in our lives when we need fear to kick us into action and run (such as a car pulling out in front of us or a lion chasing us). But when we're scared of starting a new relationship, starting a new job or deciding to change careers, telling someone we love them for the first time, booking our first ever solo trip, posting our first video onto social media or starting a new business, those fears (although seemingly very real) are not dangerous or pose a threat to our lives. But instinctively as a coping mechanism, fear tries to keep us safe and protected and tries to cling us to comfort.

Comfort in small pockets is great. I love the comfort of climbing into bed with new pyjamas and freshly washed sheets, the comfort of being home and curling up on the couch watching a movie with my favourite snacks. But when our entire lives become comfortable it becomes really hard to create change and the resistance to change becomes even stronger. So how do we push through when we want to run? How do we face fear when instinctively we have been told to listen and believe what it says to us? If new beginnings lie on the other side of fear, how do we get there?

Think of how fear shows up for you in your life. Does it tell you you're not good enough? Does it make you believe that you are not worthy of having the big vision you created for yourself? Does it tell you that you need to stay where you are – in what's comfortable? Does it tell you to say yes to that event, because if you don't go you'll let someone else down (even when you really need a quiet night to yourself)? Does it judge you, when you wear that bright piece of clothing that some may say is "too much" but to you, it makes you feel bold and empowered? Does it tell you off for eating that slice of cake? When you aren't making sales does fear tell you that you were crazy for starting your own business and that you should just give up? Does it pick out every flaw of every photo you take of yourself? Does it judge every bit of cellulite on your body?

What does fear tell you?

....
....
....
....

And what have you believed is true?

....
....
....
....

Our fears show up in the most creative ways, and although it will take every ounce of strength you have, there is a way to cross the bridge over to your new beginning. And that comes with choosing courage every single time you are faced with fear. When faced with fear, our minds are wired to conserve energy so if there is an option that will take less energy, our brains will instinctively want to choose that. It's why we feel resistance when we go to explore new things, because it physically requires more energy to form new neural pathways and step into the unknown.

Consider this example:

You're not enjoying your job but it pays well and you're really comfortable. You know everything there is to know and so you're not often challenged. You work the same hours every week and earn the same amount of money. But one day, you see a job advertised that sparks your curiosity, it sounds like a dream job. The hours are flexible but the pay is less, the opportunity you'll have to learn and be challenged and grow is there. At first, you're so excited. You rush home and do up your CV to send in. But then after a few hours, fear kicks in and whispers to you...

How will you get by with less money?
How will you know you'll enjoy it?
What happens if you suck at the job?
You probably wouldn't even get the role, how often do people find their dream role? Do you think you're worthy of having it?
This job is in a different location, you'll have to get two trains instead of one?
What if you start and no one likes you?
You should just be happy with the job you have, some people don't even have a job!

This is what fear sounds like.
So what do you choose? Do you choose to listen to what fear has to say? Or do you choose the excitement, the unknown, the uncertainty knowing that by doing this you may create space for the impossible to happen, the magic of a new beginning?
The one thing that will guide you when faced with fear, the one thing that will act as your North star and get you through the tough and uncertain times is *courage*.

"Don't ever make decisions based on fear. Make decisions based on hope and possibility. Make decisions based on what should happen, not what shouldn't."
Michelle Obama

COURAGE

"Your life is short and rare and amazing and miraculous, and you want to do really interesting things and make really interesting things while you're still here."
Elizabeth Gilbert,
Big Magic

When it comes to fear, it's less about being fearless and more about being courageous, vulnerable and opening yourself up to be seen and heard by the world. Australian nurse, Bronnie Ware spent several years working in palliative care, caring for patients in the last 12 weeks of their lives. In her book *The Top Five Regrets of The Dying*, she said the number one regret of the dying was "I wish I'd had the courage to live a life true to myself, not the life others expected of me".

In her book Ware says: "This was the most common regret of all. When people realise that their life is almost over and look back clearly on it, it is easy to see how many dreams have gone unfulfilled. Most people had not honoured even a half of their dreams and had to die knowing that it was due to choices they had made, or not made. Health brings a freedom very few realise, until they no longer have it".

The other top regrets were: I wish I hadn't worked so hard; I wish I'd had the courage to express my feelings; I wish I had stayed in touch with my friends; I wish that I had let myself be happier.

No matter what stage of life you are in, try not to have regrets. You have the ability today to do what you want to do with your life, to do what matters to you. Sometimes we need a little nudge to remind ourselves that we're not on this earth for an infinite amount of time, in fact, the only certainty we have in life is that our time is unknown and limited. What we do from today is what matters. And no matter how much living big scares you, courage will always be there guiding you along the way. Courage is not the absence of fear. Courage is simply the result of taking action despite fear.

+++

*"You can choose courage or you can choose comfort.
But you cannot have both"*
Brené Brown

+++

The topic of courage would not be complete without mentioning Dr Brené Brown. Brown's TedX talk "The Power Of Vulnerability" has over 43 million views. She has spent the past two decades studying and researching human connection, courage, vulnerability, shame and empathy and has collected over 100,000 data points. Brené talks widely about the vulnerability of courage and says "vulnerability is hard, and it's scary, and it feels dangerous. But it's not as hard or scary or dangerous as getting to the end of our lives and having to ask ourselves, 'what if I would've shown up?'"

I think that's the one question we're all afraid of answering at the end of our time. But what if we got to the end of our lives knowing that we did show up? That we did choose courage over comfort. That we did not let fear beat us and keep us small. What if we did choose to ignite our sparks and realise our full potential?

To thank Brené for her courageous and incredible work I wanted to share my favourite lessons I have learnt from her.

1. Wholehearted Living

Brené defines wholehearted living as "engaging in our lives from a place of worthiness. It means cultivating the courage, compassion, and connection to wake up in the morning and think, *no matter what gets done and how much is left undone, I am enough*. It's going to bed at night thinking, *Yes, I am imperfect and vulnerable and sometimes afraid, but that doesn't change the truth that I am also brave and worthy of love and belonging*."

Wholehearted living is showing up and letting all of you be seen by the world. It's the courage to share your story with others and having the sense of worthiness to believe that who you are is worthy and enough.

One of my most vulnerable and courageous moments was telling my partner Adrian for the first time that I loved him. It was the first time I had ever told a man that I loved him. I had always left a relationship before it got to

How can you own your story and rewrite your own ending?

....

....

....

I started my first business at 18 years old. I was eager, naive, excited and full of possibility. I saved up all my money, flew to China and found myself a manufacturer on the other side of the world. I had a design team behind me, models wearing my dresses and photographers snapping my designs. I was learning whilst I was going but I loved it. The trouble was, I really had no idea what I was doing. Over the years, I began to lose money, I lost the drive to sell my product that I had worked so hard to create. I had built up a successful following and was making traction in the fashion world, but I let the judgement of others get to me. I wasn't strong enough to push through the struggles and continue to forge ahead. I gave up on something that I was successfully growing and I quit on myself. I let my uncertainty get the better of me, and allowed anxiety to take over. As the years passed and I tried many different things, my initial failure of giving up followed me everywhere. I wanted to start another business, but I was scared I would fail again. I was scared that I'd pour my heart and soul into another project, only for it to fall over again. At this point in my life I was well and truly letting my story define me. Until eventually I decided I had to own that part of my story. I had learnt so much about running a business, the power of vision and my own growth, I realised it truly was a big part of my story.

My version of success had led me to believe I had failed when in fact, I created a vision to empower women all over the world to feel beautiful and strong and I achieved that. What I did not focus on was the messages I received from women saying how beautiful they felt when they wore my designs or the people I had inspired to go after their dreams simply by following my own.

When you look back at your story, where can you see the courage it took for you to keep going despite what happened?

....
....
....
....
....

3. Choosing Courage Over Comfort

> *"Sometimes the bravest and most important thing you can do is just show up."*
> **Brené Brown**

Courage is sometimes not a big leap forward that the heroic story is often perceived as. Sometimes courage is simply in the small ordinary moments that no one knows or hears about. Brené calls this "ordinary courage". It could be the first day at a new job, the first date after a breakup, going to the gym for the first time, booking a flight to a new country on your own.

Choosing courage is a choice that we get to make in each moment. I chose courage when I opened up to my friends and family about the anxiety and depression I was experiencing. Breaking down and talking about this experience was one of the hardest things I've had to face in my life. My identity was attached to looking and being a certain way, which was the "positive—always happy—always smiling" persona that people knew me to be. I felt everything from judgement, guilt, unworthiness, shame and weakness when I thought about opening up. It wasn't fearlessness that I needed but the courage to show up, to be open and brave enough to ask for help from the people who loved me the most.

Where have you chosen courage over comfort?

....

....

....

....

....

What have you learnt about vulnerability from these last few pages?

....

....

....

....

....

I didn't change the world through my courage, but I did change my world. I learnt that I could be stronger than ever, that I was worthy of love no matter what and that sometimes breaking down is the best way to rebuild even stronger.

If nothing else, in the moments you feel fear remember that courage is always beside you. You are worthy of having it all, of being loved, of being heard and of being seen. Don't let the world tell you anything else, you are enough, you have always been enough.

"Only those who risk going too far can possibly find out how far they can go."
T.S Eliot

OUR EMOTIONS ARE JUST AN EXPERIENCE

I want you to think back to the last time you felt a strong emotion. Were you scared, anxious, excited, happy, fearful, nervous, loving? And in that moment of feeling that emotion did you believe that you were that emotion? That you were happy, anxious, excited? I'm about to introduce a thought to you that may take some time warming up to, but when you use this thought process next time you feel strong emotions, everything will change for the better.

Eckhart Tolle said, "Rather than being your thoughts and emotions, be the awareness behind them."

You see, it's not our thoughts and emotions that define us. Emotions are simply the strong feelings we experience through our circumstances, mood or relationship with others. They are not set in stone and can change at any moment. So, we are not defined by the feelings that we have in our day – we're simply experiencing them. Experiencing anger, sadness, frustration, nervousness.

I learnt this concept through a psychologist I saw when I was going through a period of anxiety and depression.

I thought I was anxious, rather than acknowledging that I was simply experiencing anxiety at that moment in time. I told myself I was wrong for feeling the way I did, which only ended up making my situation worse.

But when I started to acknowledge that I was simply experiencing anxiety, everything shifted for me. I no longer attached that label and let feelings and emotions define who I was. I was able to rationalise the feelings much better. I could remind myself, "Oh, you're just experiencing this feeling right now, Bec. It's OK."

Something magical happened when I stopped resisting and making myself wrong for experiencing the anxiety and simply allowed it to come and go when it did. The less I fought it the more it slowly began to disappear. By becoming an observer of my emotions I was able to control them better. I had started to observe the inner dialogue and regained control over my emotions. How? By not letting the feelings define me.

Remember, every emotion we feel has a purpose. In order to appreciate the good, we sometimes have to know the bad.

Consider this:
- Without experiencing sadness, how would you know deep fulfilling happiness?
- Without experiencing anxiety, how would you know calmness?
- Without experiencing loneliness, how would you know connection?
- Without experiencing doubt, how would you know certainty?
- Without experiencing fear, how would you know courage?

OUR EMOTIONS ARE JUST AN EXPERIENCE

We are human beings having a human experience and it's the feeling of all emotions that enable us to connect, empathise and communicate with those around us. But our feelings do not define who we are. So don't let fear, doubt, worry, uncertainty or anything else stop you from moving forward in your life.

"A certain darkness is needed to see the stars."
Osho,
The Book of Secrets

STORIES

Anthropologists will tell you that storytelling is central to human existence. It allows us to share lessons, past memories and pass on important information through generations. Stories allow us to envision the impossible and to connect with others that believe what we believe. Although, we don't just tell stories to others, we also tell them to ourselves.

In *The Art of Immersion: Why Do We Tell Stories*, writer Frank Rose said, "Stories are recognizable patterns, and in those patterns we find meaning. We use stories to make sense of our world and to share that understanding with others."

So what does this have to do with facing fear, realising your potential and igniting your spark? I can tell you now, it has everything to do with it.

When an event happens in our lives we create a memory around it and store it in our brain to use for the next time something similar happens. We call this, *the event*. We don't just remember the event, we subconsciously create a story that goes with it and attach meaning to it. If the event was bad, we will do whatever it takes to prevent it from happening again. And if it was good, then we will naturally want to repeat those events.

The event can be anything from your first love, first day at school, a break up, food poisoning, the first time you failed an exam, when someone let you down or broke your trust, a time you let yourself down etc. The meaning behind the event is something psychologists call "Meaning making" which can be described as the process of how people construe, understand, or make sense of life events, relationships and the self. As humans, we create meaning out of everything. Someone looks at us a certain way – we create a story or meaning from it. After our first breakup – we create meaning around why it happened to us... it goes on and on.

What this means is that, when we make a decision on our future, we naturally refer back to our past stories. But what if we have created false stories in our head and use that to project onto our future? Well, we actually do this a lot.

Imagine the last relationship you had, your partner broke up with you. This is now the second time in a row this has happened. You create a story that either you're not good enough and future partners will break up with you, or something must be wrong with you. You shut yourself off from any new relationships to prevent yourself from being hurt.

The danger here is that, of course you want to prevent yourself from getting hurt. But it is not to say that your next relationship will be the same. You never know what's around the corner, but if you keep reliving the same story in your head you may miss out on the most incredible person who will show you that you are worthy. This is where courage and vulnerability is also needed. Because it truly does take courage to show up after being hurt.

Another example, is *the event* that happened to make you

feel not good enough for the very first time. Think back to what happened. You could have been five years old or twelve years old, like me.

One of my most memorable moments was in my second week of Phys.Ed classes at my new school, just after my parents had uprooted me and my two sisters Hannah and Katy from a small town in New Zealand to Southern Spain. I tried to walk into the girls' changing rooms before our lesson. But I was being blocked at the door by a girl named Brittany.

"Only girls can come in here," she said to me with a disapproving look.

Of course I was a girl, but I was clearly different enough for her to say that to me. I guess I knew I was different. I wasn't yet one of the cool girls in this new private school my parents had sent me to. I had a funny Kiwi accent and New Zealand seemed so foreign to people that they actually asked if we had cars or had to ride to school on horses.

I missed my friends and life back in New Zealand so much that every day I would come home in tears begging my mum to homeschool me. As the months went on, I created a story that in order to be liked I had to change. My accent started to change to fit in with everyone else and I befriended a girl named Hannah (who is still an extremely close friend to this day). Together we started wearing cool clothes, makeup, hanging out and partying with the "cool crowd" and I actually ended up becoming friends with Brittany.

For some reason, I will always remember that. Because that was the first time I tried to change myself in order to be liked. There are plenty other defining moments that happened growing up where I changed who I was, but that was the first. As small and insignificant as it seems now – I let Brittany's comment mean something about who I was that was not true. And that's the danger of the stories we create, sometimes they feel so real that we believe the stories we tell ourselves to be true. Sometimes we believe them so much that we spend the rest of our lives believing them.

Take a moment to consider what stories you've created in your own mind, based on experiences you've been through in your life. What happened to you? And what did you make that mean about who you are? How old were you when it happened? What did you feel?

I want to thank you for being brave with me and going deep. This is hard stuff, and to look into your past and face old stories and beliefs really takes something. So I acknowledge you for being courageous and I am extremely proud of you. I hope you are proud of yourself too.

When we look back at all the stories and events we created and gave meaning to, it's truly exhausting. We carry these stories around like baggage, it's heavy and does not serve us. What if everything we chose from now did not come from what we know from our past, but from a space of what's possible right now?

True freedom lies in our willingness to not be defined by our stories. To let go of the weight we're carrying with all of our meaning, stories and limiting beliefs packed inside. No matter what happened in your past, no one can take your freedom away. What you think, what you believe and what you know to be true in your heart is yours. No one has the power to change that.

*"When we are brave enough to look at our darkness.
We become courageous enough to shine our light."*
Alexi Panos

RE-WRITE AND REDEFINE

"Fear, to a great extent, is born of a story we tell ourselves, and so I chose to tell myself a different story."
Cheryl Strayed

My dad is one of the most courageous people I know. After being told one night by his teachers at parent teacher interviews that he was dumb and was never going to do any good in his life, that he would end up in prison and never amount to anything in this world — he decided to change his life.

The day after he turned 14, he left school and said to his mum, "I'm not going back to school." She replied "well, you're not going to sit around at home, so go get a job". My nanna was an incredibly strong woman, who worked hard her entire life.

The next day he started work with a guy called Phillip Hill. Philip had a big farm with dozers, tractors and he gave

Dad the opportunity to learn and to grow. Philip believed in my dad. Through Philip he learnt how to operate dozers and machinery and in that he found his passion. My dad has now travelled to over 67 countries and is the CEO of Minepro Global. Throughout his life he has inspired thousands of people through the work he does, to always do their best, take a chance on what you love and to be better. But most importantly to believe in yourself and to not let the opinions of others define the story of your life.

My dad had every odd against him. He was adopted and spent the first few months of his life in the Salvation Army orphanage as a brown Maori boy. Whilst all the other new parents chose the white babies, my nanna Nathalie Statham saw something in my dad and chose to raise him as her own son. They had very little money but she gave Dad all that she could. She believed in my dad and knew he would go on to do great things in the world. His advice when I asked him how he got through the tough periods and after being told at 13 that he would never amount to anything was this: "Fail, learn, try again and get better and better at your passion. Better yourself through learning and build on your skills. Don't be afraid to try something new and always do your best. This is what drives me still today."

How have you let the opinions of others keep you from doing what you love?

....

....

....

....

No matter what your stories have been in the past. Now is the time for you to rewrite and disrupt the way they have been running your lives. Here is how you can begin:

1. Identify the limiting stories you are telling yourself
- "I'll never be successful doing what I love."
- "I'm not smart enough or good enough."
- "Something has to give, I can't be successful, abundant and in love."

Whatever it is, dig deep. Embrace the discomfort of looking at your life from this angle. We all have stories ruling us. The difference between you and the people doing the thing that you've always wanted to do, is simply the stories you and they tell themselves.

2. Flip Your Narrative
Once you've identified the story, it's time to create a new one that counteracts your previous limiting beliefs. These new stories will support the life you want to create!

For example:
- "I can be successful doing what I love because no one else in the world is me and has my unique talents."
- "I am enough and I have always been enough."
- "I am worthy of living my dream life."

Consider how can you change your story that counteracts your current state of living, to one that is more empowering and aligns with the life you know you are worthy of having.

3. Practise
Like anything, you need to flex this muscle.
When you've been living a certain way for a number of

years you're going to feel resistance to change and it might feel like you're lying to yourself at the start. When in fact, the story is the lie because you have been using events that happened in the past to predict your future. The only way to grow stronger muscles is to break down the muscle fibres in order for them to regrow stronger, that's why you feel sore after a workout. Break down your story, embrace the resistance to change and growing pains that come with doing anything new. This is the path to your true self. You are capable of anything and you are so much stronger than you know.

4. Supporting a New Story
Reaffirming a new story in itself isn't enough. To push past the resistance, you have to believe it and look at areas of your life for evidence that it's true. Look at your life. What have you achieved? When have you pushed through when times have been tough? When have you proved to yourself that you can do it? What do you know to be true about yourself?

If you cannot find evidence. Then take action to write your new story, and use that to reaffirm it's possible. You are worthy because you are here on earth. Sometimes that is all the evidence you need.

If it helps, get creative and visual and write these new empowering statements somewhere you can see them. Often, we focus so much on the negative stories that we forget to look at the moments where we have absolutely nailed it! Think back to what you are most proud of.

What were you doing? How did that make you feel? Create your evidence case! Where our focus goes, energy flows.

5. Take Action
Now that you have a new story, have the courage to try things you've never done before and open your eyes to the opportunities that are shining bright in front of you. Believing and hoping isn't enough. You've got to move and take steps forward. It doesn't matter if you get knocked down, or an old belief creeps in. Catch it and know that it's just a story.

You get to decide what you're going to stand for. Take a stand for the most authentic and courageous version of yourself. Go after those dreams, and don't ever let a story of who you thought you were hold you back from living your best life ever again.

There is a legend from Cherokee, a tribe of indigenous people of the Southeastern Woodlands, USA. A Cherokee grandfather tells his grandson about the internal fight going on inside him between two wolves. One is evil and the other is good. The one that becomes more powerful is the one he feeds.

What I love about this story is the message of the one we feed becomes more powerful. I invite you to look at what stories you've been feeding. There are some stories that will empower you, but others are holding you back and limiting who you can be. Remember that your existence on earth is a miracle in itself and that you are capable of achieving absolutely anything. By rewriting your stories, you will rewrite your life. You have the power to create the change you want at any moment, if you have the courage to look at the parts of yourself that no longer serve you.

You cannot erase the past. But from this moment on you can own the story that's already been written, let go of what no longer serves you, grab a pen and rewrite the next chapters of your life.

"You gain strength, courage, and confidence by every experience in which you really stop to look fear in the face. You must do the thing which you think you cannot do."
Eleanor Roosevelt

WHAT'S YOUR GLASS CEILING?

"In my life, I've discovered that if I cling to the notion that something's not possible, I'm arguing in favor of limitation. And if I argue for my limitations, I get to keep them."
Gay Hendricks

It's not only stories that hold us back from greatness. We have subconsciously created our own internal glass ceiling that limits us in some way shape or form. Gay Hendricks, author of *The Big Leap* calls this "The Upper Limit Problem". He believes that we have this subconscious idea of how much happiness we deserve and that we tend to sabotage our success when we reach our own upper limits. The reality is that when you take unapologetic bold action you are always going to come up against upper limits. So, what do you do when they show up in your life?

I want you to imagine a glass ceiling a few metres above your head. That ceiling was programmed when you were young and determines the amount of love, success, creativity and abundance you think you're worthy of receiving. Once you start to have huge success in any of those areas, you eventually hit the ceiling and are unable to progress to the next level because of your limiting beliefs. Fear strikes once again! Now although this is an imaginary glass ceiling the concept of Upper Limiting is very real.

Can you think back to a time things were going really well for you and suddenly you began to sabotage your success?

For example:
- You saved more money than ever but splurged on something unnecessary to bring you back to the 'normal' level of savings you're accustomed to?
- Your relationship is going incredibly well – too well – so you look for problems when there aren't really any? You may start an argument for no reason or deliberately push your partner's buttons.
- You're on a new healthy diet and feeling great, but you sabotage your progress with a cheat meal which quickly turns into a cheat day, then a cheat week, then eventually a bad month? Before you know it, the diet is over and you're right back where you started.
- Your business is thriving and growing but then all of a sudden you start questioning yourself and fearing something bad might happen? *Can I really do this? Have I just been lucky to get this far?*

These are all examples limiting beliefs that can trigger when you hit your glass ceiling. Another concept known as the 'Happiness Set Point' also relates to the concept of Upper Limiting. In her book, *Happy For No Reason*, Psychologist Marci Shimoff says that, "Researchers have found that no matter what happens to you in life, you tend to return to a fixed range of happiness. Like your weight set-point, which keeps the scale hovering around the same number, your happiness set-point will remain the same unless you make a concerted effort to change it."

Shimoff continues: "In fact, there was a famous study conducted that tracked people who'd won the lottery — what many people think of as the ticket to the magic kingdom of joy. Within a year, these lucky winners returned to approximately the same level of happiness they'd experienced before their windfall. Surprisingly, the same was true for people who became paraplegic. Within a year or so of being disabled, they also returned to their original happiness level."

So not only do you have a glass ceiling that you need to break through, but you now have a Happiness Set Point too? Hey, I never said igniting your spark was going to be easy! But it can be done. So, let's talk in the next chapter about how we can get you through that ceiling.

+++

> *"When we love, we always strive to become better than we are. When we strive to become better than we are, everything around us becomes better too."*
> **Paulo Coelho,**
> **The Alchemist**

"Live the Life of Your Dreams: Be brave enough to live the life of your dreams according to your vision and purpose instead of the expectations and opinions of others."
Roy T Bennett,
The Light in the Heart

BREAK THAT CEILING!

When you reach your upper limit, be prepared for everything to come at you — sickness, fear, self-limiting beliefs, not wanting to leave your family behind in your success, fear of being too much, fear of not being enough. The more you push that glass ceiling, the more you may experience!

So, can it be done? Absolutely. And here's how you can start to push through that ceiling.

1. Challenge your beliefs: Next time you find yourself thinking "I can't afford that", "I'll always be this weight", "I'll never make an income doing what I love", "I am so happy right now that something will probably go wrong soon", ask yourself where that belief came from? Think back to when that belief was formed and challenge the actual truth of it. Catch it before it catches you. Is there anything you can think of? Write it down now.

....

....

2. Get rid of the noise: Whilst you cannot control all the thoughts that come into your mind, you do choose whether to pay attention to them. Try not to engage in limiting beliefs. Ask yourself, "does this thought take me closer to who I want to be and the life I am creating?" If the answer is no, push it to the side and focus on what makes you come alive.

3. Cultivate an attitude of gratitude: No matter how bad things are going, there is always something small you can be grateful for. Whisper "thank you" when something great happens. Appreciate a beautiful sunny day. Find lessons in adversity. Use gratitude to your advantage and always have an open and willing mindset.
Appreciating what you have right now, opens up space for more to come in. If you can't appreciate what you have right now, nothing will ever be good enough for you. Make gratitude a daily practice.

Can you think of five things you are grateful for right now? Write them down below.

4. Believe: Believe that no matter what, you are worthy of all of the success, love and financial abundance in the world. An upper limit is simply a story, so don't let it define who you are.

I'll let you in on a little secret – there is absolutely no right or wrong way to push through the ceiling. Do what works for you. You just simply need to keep taking action. Do you want to be someone that played at 100% and gave it your all regardless of fear? Or do you want to be someone who tries to do something but lets fear win?

Often, it's the paths of uncertainty, fear and resistance that offer us the greatest opportunities to grow. And the more we tread down these paths, the more we gain clarity on what it is we do love, we find excitement in the unknown and our tolerance to change strengthens. Consider your first date, your first time speaking in public or your first day at work. You probably experienced uncertainty, nerves and maybe even felt like you didn't want to turn up. Regardless of the outcome, you did it. And when you do something once, you can do it over and over again.

If nothing else, remember this:

> **SMALL LIFE =**
> Always staying within the limits of what's comfortable, but always in doubt of what could have been if you'd ventured out of your comfort zone.
>
> **LIFE OF IGNITING YOUR SPARK =**
> Fear, excitement, failure, passion, adventure, uncertainty, creating the life you want and unapologetically going after your dreams.

"Sometimes we just simply have to find a way. The moment we decide to fulfil something, we can do anything."
Greta Thunberg

YOUR GOLDEN TRUTH

"Let yourself be drawn by the strange pull of what you love. It will not lead you astray."
Rumi

When you shine bright in to the world, you unintentionally can cast a shadow on those who are not shining their lights. So many people desperately want to change, but they aren't willing to do what it takes. And so, when someone close to them starts to change, they feel uncomfortable and can try to bring them back down to their own level of comfort.

I once heard a saying that said, "Sometimes you have to let go of half of what you are, in order to become twice the person you can become." Like a caterpillar before it turns into a beautiful butterfly and spreads its wings. You have to be able to let go of old stories, environments, habits and sometimes even people around you in order to blossom into the person you need to become.

Living your truth is the most courageous thing you can do. You have spent your life being somebody else's version of who they think you should be for the world, now is the time for you to go and discover who the *real you* truly is.

Jack Canfield, author of *Chicken Soup for the Soul*, said that "The greatest wound we've all experienced is somehow being rejected for being our authentic self. And as a result of that, we then try to be what we're not to get approval, love, protection, safety, money, whatever that is. And the real need for all of us really is to reconnect with the essence of who we really are. Re-own all the disowned parts of ourselves, whether it's our emotions, our spirituality, whatever. We all go around hiding parts of ourselves."

Canfield then went on to share his experience with a Buddhist teacher who said to him, "Here's the secret: If you were to meditate for 20 years, this is where you'd finally get: to just be yourself, but be all of you."

Just be yourself – but be all of you.

Now that we've just saved ourselves 20 years of meditation, it's time for you to be yourself – all of you. To stop being somebody else's version of who they think you should be. And to be your true self. Your imperfections, your quirks, your laughter and crazy ideas, the world needs them. The world needs more trailblazers, disrupters, rule-breakers, visionaries, realness and imperfect action, and we need less perfection, judgement, resistance, assumptions, limiting beliefs, rules, gossip and expectations about how we should live our lives.

In the words of 19th century Philosopher Ralph Waldo Emerson, "To be yourself in a world that is constantly trying to make you something else is the greatest accomplishment."

Keep shinning bright, peeling back the layers and

connecting with what matters to you.

Go out there, break some rules and shine your light bright into the world.

"Start before you feel ready. You don't need to know where it's all going. You'll work it out along the way."
**Rebecca Campbell,
Light Is the New Black**

Part 3:

Brave Action

"We have forgotten that courage is a choice, and that permission to move forward with boldness is never given by the fearful masses. Most have forgotten that seeking change always requires a touch of insanity. If taking action before the perfect conditions arise, or before we receive permission, is unreasonable or reckless, then we must be unreasonable and reckless. We must remember we are not the sum of our intentions but of our action."
Brendon Burchard,
The Motivation Manifesto

EL CAMINO DE SANTIAGO

"It's your road, and yours alone. Others may walk it with you, but no one can walk it for you."
Rumi

In 2016, I walked the Camino De Santiago with my mum and two sisters Hannah and Katy. My mum, Joanna was about to walk her Camino for the fifth time and so I decided to join her. I was at a crossroads in my life and had heard the incredible soul-searching adventure the Camino promised. The Camino De Santiago is a 800 km pilgrimage that stretches from the top of Spain bordering the French Pyrenees to Santiago de Compostela. In 2018, 320,000 pilgrims from all over the world came to walk their Camino.

Everyone walking the path is called a pilgrim regardless of whether they're doing it for religious, spiritual or adventure reasons. They say that pilgrims do the Camino like they "do life". Someone who is extremely driven and a high-achiever, will often push themselves to go farther and faster than they should and suffer physical problems. And those that go to "escape life" often find themselves facing their life and dealing with thoughts and feelings they have suppressed inside. The Camino is walked all year round, it's not a race but a journey. Below are some words from my mum on what the Camino meant for her.

"El Camino de Santiago translates into English as Way of Saint James. This ancient pilgrimage journey with various starting points leading to the shrine of the apostle Saint James the Great in the cathedral of Santiago de Compostela in Galicia in north western Spain. It is said that the remains of the saint are buried there.

However, the Camino is more than another trip on your bucket-list, it's a spiritual journey. It's a very personal expedition from the moment you decide you want to undertake it, and there really is no end-point. It's not like you get to the cathedral and all the wisdom and divine answers suddenly appear. It's more of an awakening of your purpose and you start to see life more clearly along with realising what is really important to you. Part of this is the simple life you experience on the Camino; disposable sheets, simple meals like bread and soup and 5 euro per night hostels coupled with limited wifi. Sometimes decluttering your life for this period of time and carrying all your needs on your back brings a clarity you would never usually have. It's a time for reflection, connection and introspection. It's definitely life-changing".

Joanna Statham

The Camino was truly life-changing but also a reminder that what we seek is not out for us to find but already found inside our own hearts. I walked and I walked and I walked. I walked so much that I ran out of things to think about and sometimes the road would be so long that I didn't pass or see anyone for a few hours. In those moments, all that is left is your own thoughts. When I finally faced my inner thoughts and feelings I realised that I had come here to escape. Escape from the relationships I had in life that were no longer serving me, escape from the job I no longer enjoyed and the life I was currently living. Walking the Camino truly transformed my perspective on the life I was living. Everything became simple and all I had to focus on was walking one foot in front of the other. I stopped caring about what I looked like to others, being liked by the strangers I met or trying to keep up with people who walked faster than me. I walked my own Camino – at my pace. Something I hadn't done in a very long time.

Everyone I met was on their own journey, their own walk, their own Camino —all trying to find their way. Every turn off the road you would see a yellow arrow telling you that you are on the right path. And every pilgrim you passed, would smile and say "Buen Camino" which means "good walk" which really symbolized "good journey". Buen Camino is truly symbolic of the path we all take, because we are all in this incredible journey of walking our own Camino. One night over dinner I met an older lady from Cape Town who turned and said to me "The Camino starts when you get home". This whole time I had been walking to Santiago De Compostela, getting closer and closer to my destination each and every day. But the real walk, the real journey began when I got home.

Here are some posts I found on Instagram that I wrote along the way:

21st April 2016
Everywhere you go there are signs leading the way.

+++

21 April 2016
I stopped for lunch and started speaking to an old Spanish man who was selling crystals on the road. When I left to continue walking he handed me a serviette and wished me "Suerte" which translates to luck. I walked on and opened up the serviette to find this. My lessons today is that the way is always guided.

22 April 2016
Too exhausted to upload photos but I have to share this one. About 12 km into our Camino today and we found a big mountain of stones. People come and place a stone as a reflection of their burdens they are leaving behind. One of the main reasons people walk the Camino is to let go and find their way.

+++

22nd April 2016
This is what the Camino really feels like. Only 2 km from finishing for the day with throbbing pain in our feet after climbing 26 km over rocky terrain, so we laid on the side of a mountain and laughed and ate.

23rd April 2016
Every day there are so many ups and downs. One minute you're warm, full and dry and laughing and the next there's torrential rain and you're freezing. As tough as it gets it's always okay.

+++

2016
Somewhere along the way.

25th April 2016
Today was incredible Many ups and downs but a sense of freedom and letting go was experienced too. Laughing, hurting, crying, sun, wind, cold. And that's just in the hour! The more I go into the Camino, the less consumed I feel. So much shows up and it's because I'm so present in the moment. My focus isn't on a job my weekend or next weekend. It's one step at a time. The next village. The next few kilometres to walk.

+++

27th April 2016
We always get to our destination but it's how we got there that matters most.

+++

27th April 2016
I am the Camino. I am the truth. I am life.
What I have found is that the Camino gives you exactly what you need. The right people. The right journey. The right conditions. Everything.
Buen Camino.

ACTION

"When you dance, your purpose is not to get to a certain place on the floor. It's to enjoy each step along the way."
Dr Wayne Dyer

Igniting Your Spark and realising your potential starts with a vision and connecting to what matters to you. It begins with noticing what excites you and what you're curious about.

We began this book by drafting our WHY statement. Our bold statement that we could align with. The next big part focused on fear and courage. What it meant to choose courage over comfort and how to catch the stories we have been living with. And now, after building our foundations it's time to share our magic with the world and take action. Most people take years and years preparing to take action. They wait and wait for the right time, the right moment, the right circumstances, the right mindset.

I envision action as the movement between the match

and the matchbox. The match itself cannot ignite the spark, it has to move forward to ignite the spark. Like the match, so do you. Knowing your vision is not enough. Knowing how to face your fears and choosing courage is not enough. Just like action on its own isn't enough. But when these three come together, that's when the magic happens.

The first step to taking action is to simply start. To step forward in a direction. As the ancient philosopher Lao Tzu said, "The journey of a thousand miles begins with a single step". Notice Lao Tzu doesn't say the step needs to be perfect or large. It can be a small step, an imperfect step, so long as it's a step forward.

We truly do have the power to pave our own way in the world and although exciting and equally fearful, with courage and belief you will get stronger and stronger as you walk towards the distance of what matters most to you.

JK Rowling said, "It is impossible to live without failing at something, unless you live so cautiously that you might as well not have lived at all – in which case, you fail by default." And she's right. By letting the fear of what could happen stop you from taking any action, you fail regardless. So you may as well go all in, and see what happens. Jim Carrey beautifully said, "I learned many great lessons from my father, not the least of which, was that you can fail at what you don't want so you might as well take a chance on doing what you love"

How often have you taken no action due to the fear of failing?

....

....

So what's left in your way?
Is fear lingering around disguised?

Has the logic of your brain kicked in and come up with one million great sounding excuses as to why you cannot take action?

Start to understand the inner workings of your mind. Observe what's happening and find freedom in acting regardless. Stagnation has always scared me, things staying the same and not experiencing the fullness of what's possible in my life. So action has been a key thing for me and I can honestly tell you that I have failed forward in most areas of my life.

The question I ask is: are you willing to fail forward?

"Quit hiding your magic. The world is ready for you."
Danielle Doby

WHO ARE YOU GOING TO BE?

"You have treasures hidden within you – extraordinary treasures – and so do I, and so does everyone around us. And bringing those treasures to light takes work and faith and focus and courage and hours of devotion, and the clock is ticking, and the world is spinning, and we simply do not have time anymore to think so small."
Elizabeth Gilbert,
Big Magic

Our vision is clear, our belief is stronger than ever, we know we have to take imperfect action, so what's next?

It's the final stretch, but there is still work to be done. Everything we have covered so far has prepared you for what's to come. Now is the time you are going to decide who you are going to be, what actions you need to do, in order to have the life you envision.

Previous to today you may have been operating the other

way around. You may have said to yourself, "When I *have* this, then I'll *do* this, and then I'll finally *be* this."

For example, "When I get a promotion, then I'll finally act more senior and then I'll finally be happy". Or maybe "When I finally lose 10 kilos, then I'll feel confident enough to go to the gym and I'll finally love my body." But this way of thinking and being does not work because everything external has to change in order for us to act and be happy.

When you start to ask yourself, who do I need to BE today? And If I was BEing those qualities, what would I do? What actions would I take? This is the true formula to taking inspired imperfect action and making your dreams become a reality.

I used to believe that I had to lose a certain amount of weight before I could love and appreciate my body. So I deprived my body, hated the way I looked in the mirror and would eat barely anything during the day and then at night I would head to the cupboards and binge eat all there was. This resulted in me putting on more weight. Until one day, I learnt this concept and thought to myself. What would someone who loved their body do today? Well, they probably wouldn't starve themselves, they would probably tell themselves they were beautiful no matter what size they were, they would eat to feel good and thrive, and they would move their body in a way that made them feel good about themselves. I started to take action every day towards loving my body and before I knew it, the weight had shifted and I had the body I had always wanted. But, I didn't wait to get the body before I started to love it. The moment I decided to love my body regardless of the bumps and extra weight I was carrying was the moment I had won.

Ask yourself, who would the person who had my absolute dream life BE today? (Etc, committed, curious, passionate, excited...)

....

....

....

....

Now, commit yourself to embodying those traits into your life. Wake up in the morning and decide that today you are going to BE what you wrote above in your list.

Act as if, you already have what you truly desire and be grateful for everything that happens. You have to believe though and ensure your actions align with your beliefs. If you say you want one thing, but then go and do something completely different then the universe will not give you what you want.

But if you believe it to be true and start acting as if you already have what it is you desire, then anything is possible.

"We do not need magic to transform our world. We carry all of the power we need inside ourselves already."
J.K. Rowling

YOUR RELATIONSHIP WITH MONEY

I'm going to keep this short, because I am no money expert. But I feel it's important that we look at money. Money has enabled me to travel the world, move countries and cities multiple times and invest over $60,000 into self-development and business and on top of that write a book all at 25 years old. Now, that may not seem a lot to you, or it may seem a lot to you. The amount doesn't really matter, the principles remain the same.

I did not grow up in wealth, but I was very lucky to grow up with experiences. Money to me is simply a form of value exchange. If I wanted to fly to Europe and visit my family, I would need to look at where I was investing my money and prioritise the trip. When I was younger, my friends would say to me, I wish I was like you and could go and travel the world but I can't afford it. But if I looked at how they spent their money, they had the exact same amount as me but choose to spend it on partying or buying nice clothes.

The trip to Europe to visit my family meant more to me than nights out drinking or the nice clothes, and when I started to invest in myself and my business the same principles applied. I love the idea of beautiful luxurious clothes, expensive jewellery and jetting off to Bali on holiday every few months, but I also know those things are short-term, they're great at first but eventually the shine wears off. Whereas if I invest in myself or in a business idea, my life changes. I learn something about myself that I never knew. I connect with incredible people who also value their own growth and development. To me, that is true value.

I also work hard for the money I earn, so it's important for me to invest in things that make me feel good. And yeah, sometimes that means investing in a $7 organic almond cappuccino, or a pair of Lululemon leggings that make me feel incredible whilst working out or a massage after a long week. But these are luxuries to me and I never take them for granted. I spend money on what will grow and uplift me to get me to the next level. On the flip side, don't be afraid to invest and to spend. If your money mindset is very frugal you will forever be saving and feeling as though you don't have enough. If you always believe you don't have enough, whether you do or don't—that will be your future. Remember that you are your greatest investment. Invest in you, in your growth and what makes you happy (and if that's a beautiful piece of clothing once in a while, then go for it).

What is your relationship with money?

....

....

....

....

Aside from covering the basics of food, rent and bills, where do you spend your money?

....
....
....
....

Does it give you back an equal amount of value (if not more?). If not, how can you make more conscious choices to ensure you do get equal or more value out of your investments?

....
....
....
....

"You will grow and evolve because of your willingness to fail, to suck, to navigate murky waters, and to trust regardless of what happens."
Peta Kelly,
Earth is Hiring

SETTING YOURSELF UP FOR SUCCESS

Simply deciding that you're going to *Ignite Your Spark* and go after your biggest and boldest dreams is one of the most exciting, courageous and bravest things you can do. Most people don't fully decide to go all in. They may be curious about creating a change in an area of their life, but their words and actions display something different.

When you truly decide to go all in, give yourself the permission to do everything you can to set yourself up to succeed. One of my favourite tools has been to take ownership of my environment and redesign it.

The thing with motivation and inspiration is that it's very short-lived. I have notebook after notebook of ideas scribbled during times that I've felt inspired to act. I have made promise after promise to attend the gym first thing in the morning, and when morning rolls around, I've seemingly changed my mind. Can you relate? Have you told yourself you will do something because you feel good in the moment and only a few hours later decided you were too tired, too busy, too stressed or simply didn't feel like it anymore? What many people don't understand is that passion and motivation is the result of action. You normally don't know how you feel about something until you've done it.

A few years ago, I committed to transforming my body. And boy, was I good at excuses come morning. To combat this, I decided to lay my shoes beside my bed, pack my bag the night before and sleep in my gym gear – strange I know, uncomfortable yes, but hey it worked! When I woke, all I needed to do was put my shoes on and get out the door. I set myself up for success!

So, how can we redesign our environments to ensure we take action? How can we find inspiration and motivation to keep going? How can we set ourselves up for success?

I believe our environment has a huge impact on us. And everyone is different. If you walk into the office of Lululemon there's a certain feeling you experience. You see these beautiful people full of energy, vibrancy, smiling and looking amazing in their Lululemon workout gear. The office has a state-of-the-art gym, incredible facilities and their vision is plastered all over the walls for you to feel inspired and motivated to act. Same goes with companies like Google, Walt Disney, Swisse. They all have a certain vibe when you walk into their workspace that has been designed to enhance their employee and customer experience.

My role at Momenton, a consultancy that empowers the modern enterprise through technology and enables impactful change throughout Australia, is to look after all things People, Capability and Company Culture. It also includes designing our Culture plan which is essentially designing a plan to enhance the wellbeing and experience that our people have whilst in this company.

Below are some of my learnings and takeaways on redesigning your own environment for whatever big goal you want to achieve.

1. *What makes you feel good?* Understanding that feeling good is key to any success. We are all extremely different and work well in different scenarios. You may thrive working in a cool cafe with music pumping and the smell of coffee wafting, or a fun co-working space filled with interesting people with their own story to share. Or you may thrive in a secluded quiet space with no distractions in order to give your full undivided attention to your work. There is no right or wrong way. Get curious to how you work best and use that to your advantage.

2. *Nourish.* You can only give so much energy to your ideas, visions and others before you need to refuel. Get curious about what makes your body and mind feel nourished. Meditation, healthy eating, rest and movement are all common ways but what feels good to you? What makes you feel like you can do anything?

3. *Connect to your vision daily.* There's a reason why companies like Lululemon are so successful. They connect to their vision daily, they live and breathe their values and every decision they make and act on, stems from this. Live and breathe your vision, bring it into existence every opportunity you can. Share what you're up to with others. Build a vision board to remind yourself of your vision every day. Put it on your phone screen, post it on your social media platforms, look at it every morning when you wake up and every night before you go to sleep.

4. Redesign your space. Is your desk messy, cluttered, boring, uninspiring? If so, redesign it! Get an oil diffuser and blend uplifting oils, burn a beautiful candle, put your vision where you can see it every time you go to work. Put quotes that inspire, motivate and remind you of the bigger picture. Take a weekend to do this, buy some beautiful stationary, planners, fresh flowers, warm lighting, whatever you need. Sometimes it's the smallest things that make the biggest difference.

5. Be the change you wish to see. Sometimes our environments can be toxic, filled with negativity, gossip, judgement. Although you can't always escape these environments you can be a beacon of change. You can choose to show up regardless, to take a stand for the change you want to see. Sometimes, all that's needed is someone who is brave enough and willing enough to go first. To call out the toxicity that's sweeping through your work space, family space or friendships. Remember that you have a choice in each moment to be a part of something or stand against it.

Igniting Your Spark won't always be easy, I want to be real and honest about this. Throughout the years that I have launched businesses and stayed true to myself and my beliefs, I know there have been people judging me behind my back, laughing at me, not understanding why I won't just fit in like the others. But I choose to be me, to shine bright and to share what I stand for with others.

Many people are too afraid to step into their truth, too comfortable doing what they've always done and too attached to their identity and status. And when people are afraid, comfortable and attached to a certain way of being, they may do things, say things and try to hold others back from stepping into their greatness.

Whenever I have experienced these types of people I try to remind myself that everyone is doing the best they can with the knowledge they have. We all have incredible magic inside of us and some of us will go forth and uncover and share our magic whilst others will not. Find others that believe in you, that believe in what you stand for and believe that anything is possible. When the opportunity arises, believe in others and ignite the spark in the people around you. Be ruthless with your environment and look after it. Beware of what sucks and drains your energy and ensure that no matter what, you don't let your external environment impact your light. Don't ever stop shinning it bright.

Self-Care
In 2018, I started a project called "The Self Love Project". The intention was to redefine what self-love and self-care meant, because as I uncovered it meant different things to different people. It wasn't all massages and self-indulgence; for some people it was being unapologetic with decisions, for others, saying 'no' more than 'yes', or eating a full plate of pancakes on a Monday morning. Some needed to quit the job that drained the life out of them whilst others needed to indulge their creativity.

We give so much of ourselves on a daily basis, it is so important to refuel and give back to ourselves too. If you are a natural giver, an empath and someone who cares deeply, you will find that you naturally take on other people's energy, emotions and feelings. If this is you, which I have a feeling it is, it is absolutely essential that you have a self-care toolkit that you can refer back to when you need to refuel your body, mind and soul.

Sometimes my self-care is just mindlessly scrolling on

instagram! There... I said it! Sometimes all I want to do after a huge day is to switch off my brain and have a good scroll. Sometimes it's hanging on the couch with my favourite popcorn and a movie. It's YOUR self-care practice. It doesn't have to be facials, massages and manicures (although it can be if you want it to!). It could be ten minutes to yourself to eat your favourite meal. It could be gathering a group of your best friends and spending time with them!

Throughout the years, I have cultivated many different practices and little rituals which I will share with you. Although, I want you to go and build you own toolkit. This is your own sacred practice and what fills me up may not work for you. Go explore and discover what makes you thrive and feel incredible. We all have different budgets, timelines, needs and different things that make us happy.

I've listed below some of my current favourite self-care tools that help uplift me and equally calm me. I am a highly creative, excited individual and if I don't balance calm in there I can easily become anxious and unbalanced. After this, you are going to create your very own toolkit so be open to exploring new things and remember that this is your own practice, no one else's.

Self-Care Tools for Uplifting!

1. *Dancing!* I LOVE to put on a feel-good song and dance! It's so good for your body and soul and makes you feel truly incredible.

2. *Dry brushing.* I don't do this every morning, but the more I incorporate this into my mornings the better I feel. Dry brushing is this incredible technique whereby you use a dry bristle brush and brush your body in circular movements up towards your heart. It helps detoxify your body by increasing blood circulation and promoting lymph flow and drainage. Dry brushing also unclogs pores in the exfoliation process, which makes you feel invigorated afterwards. It's best done in the morning before a shower and takes around five minutes to do. You can buy the brushes in most chemists, pharmacies and health food stores!

3. *Exploring and working from cool cafes.* Maybe it's a Melbourne thing, but there's something I love about taking myself to a cool cafe, with an awesome vibe and sitting down and ordering my favourite coffee. It's small, but something I thrive off and love.

4. *Exercise and rest.* I've bundled these together because I would be inauthentic for saying I exercise all the time. Sometimes all my body needs is rest, and sometimes it craves movement. Over the years of pushing my body to the max, over-exercising, not exercising enough, I've learnt to honour the rhythms and signs of my body and I encourage you to do the same!

5. *Connecting with incredible people.* This is one of my favourite ways of feeling inspired and uplifted. People are bloody incredible and there is nothing like sitting down with someone and sharing a vision, hearing what excites them or what they're up to. Even just talking about what's possible, I love these conversations. They give me so much inspiration and energy to go out there and do my thing! Sometimes our friends only see a certain side of us, as do our work colleagues and family. But when you connect with people who see what you see and have similar values and interests, you get to feed off each other's energy, it's truly infectious!

* If you don't yet know of anyone to do this with, listen to podcasts, attend events that interest you, read books like you're doing now or reach out to someone who inspires you and let them know who they are for you!

6. Visioning. Anyone that comes over to my house knows that I am obsessed with having positive affirmations around me. It's the subtle reminders, statements on what I stand for, images of places I'm still yet to explore; these little reminders keep me on track.

7. Essential oils. I used to think of essential oils as a calming tool, but there are some incredible uplifting oils out there too. I use a doTERRA blend called Elevation, which is a blend of oils to promote positive mood and confidence. I diffuse this, rub it on my heart and inhale it!

8. Honouring my word. Last but not least, honouring my words is a self-care tool I have recently been implementing and it's not an easy one. Unwavering commitment. Doing the hard work and committing to getting what's needed to be done. My commitment to my dreams, visions and goals does inspire me. The more action I take, the more I am committed to getting it done! By committing to what I set for myself, I honour my word.

Self-care tools for Calming

1. Pre-shower Abhyanga. I first learnt about Abhyangas from an Indian Ayurvedic doctor. I'll share with you my version of what I do, but feel free to do more research on these as they can vary. Abhyanga is simple massaging of the body towards the direction of the movement of arterial blood. I often self-massage before I shower at night (no time for this in the morning). I use avocado oil and lather this all over my body. Sometimes I envision that this is a protection layer and envision the oil protecting me from the day's events. Abhyangas are calming for your nerves, help increase circulation in the body and is really nourishing for your skin and body, it also helps you sleep better at night.

2. Hugs. Who doesn't love a good hug? Hugs are so therapeutic, not to mention the dopamine hit we get from hugging. Whenever I feel a bit anxious or need calming, hugs are incredibly calming. If you don't have anyone to hug, remember that you always have yourself. You are your biggest companion, your biggest hero, are you will always be there for yourself. So don't be afraid to wrap your arms around yourself and give yourself a big squeeze. You are worthy of all the love and hugs in the world. Don't ever forget that.

3. *Essential oils.* I love to diffuse a doTERRA peace blend that consists of Vetiver, Lavender, Ylang Ylang, Frankincense, Clary Sage, Marjoram, Labdanum and Spearmint. This combination has been designed to promote feelings of contentment, composure and reassurance when anxious feelings overwhelm you. I also rub some lavender oil onto my heart and the soles of my feet and inhale the scent before bed.

4. *Alone time.* I am a real introvert at heart, Sure, I thrive off people, big visions and connections but I take a lot on and need time to recharge. Sometimes I lay on my bed, nap, read and listen to beautiful meditations like Sarah Blondin's - Loving and Listening to Yourself on Insight timer (you can dowload Insight timer from the app store). It's an incredible reminder to love and listen to yourself.

5. *Time with good people:* People that remind me of who I am, people with whom I can be 100% myself around, whatever that looks like.

Remember: Your self-care routine is yours, whatever makes you feel good. Whether that's a delicious plate of pancakes, a green organic smoothie or a good old Insta scroll, whatever is YOUR way of recharging, do that.

How can you redesign your environment?

....
....
....
....

And if someone was to ask you to build a self-care toolkit, what would you include?

- ....
- ....
- ....
- ....
- ....
- ....
- ....
- ....
- ....
- ....

Remember that you can always control your inner world, your thoughts, your daily habits and what you do from this day on. Don't ever forget the power you have to change your world. But don't get so lost in the vision that you forget to take a small step forward. One habit at a time, one small move towards your goal, that's all you need.

Start with the decision, and once you have chosen to act — set yourself up for success. Do whatever you can and whatever works for you. Keep recharging, keep stepping forward, keep going.

You've got what it takes, you have the tools, you've made the decision to act, anything is possible from here.

*"The biggest adventure you can take is to
live the life of your dreams."*
Oprah Winfrey

CHOOSING YOUR HARD

Anything worth doing in this life will have its challenges, and the sooner we come to terms with this, the sooner we can push forward towards our dreams.

I'd like to share with you a principle that I call "choosing my hard." In essence, this principle is a reminder that there will be difficulty on any road you choose to take in life, but it's up to you to pick which version of "hard" you want more. With everything there is a choice. You can choose the hard of growth, failing forward, learning something new and stepping outside of your comfort zone. Or the hard of stagnation, regret and never truly realising your full potential. I'll share with you a story of how I came to learn about this.

My whole life, I've felt like I've been wired differently to most. Imagination and dreaming big, never really was an issue for me. But some things aren't my strength and that's decisiveness on ideas and commitment.

A lot of my life involved moving around the world so adapting and communicating became my strength. I didn't necessarily learn the tools of commitment and pushing through when the going got tough. So, when an idea started to become too hard or I lost inspiration I would leave for the next thing. This left me in a vicious cycle where I was forever chasing the next shiny thing in front of me, it was like running in a large hamster wheel continually chasing but never moving forward.

Have you ever jumped from one idea to the next as quickly as I have in my life?

What were you running from?

There comes a moment in our lives, when we get sick and tired of the same patterns showing up. For me, I realised I was being incongruent with what I believed in and something had to change. I knew with Ignite & Co it would be different and it would start with a book. A book written to ignite spark in the lives of others. This book would be the start of something new and an ode to every single idea, vision or dream that I had ever gone after.

I knew I wanted to run my own business, and inspire beautiful, like-minded people around the world to pursue their dreams, but I had no idea how to do it. I had all the passion in the world, but I was lacking discipline and structure. I see myself more as the "organised chaos" type of woman. But in order to take my idea of building Ignite & Co seriously, I had to change that and be willing to commit to the hard.

Writing this book has involved pushing through the very resistance that has held me back for so long. For me, it comes down to perfection and things looking a certain way. My idea for this book involved luxurious paper, incredible visuals and quotes plastered everywhere. But I spent months being distracted by the design of it that I had forgotten the very purpose of why I had started writing. I wasn't writing about how to be a great designer, I was writing about igniting your spark and living a bold and courageous life! But there I was, stuck in my own bubble of perfection and the way I was going, this book nearly wasn't written at all. In fact, if It hadn't been for a man called Grant Cardone you may have never have been reading these words.

If you don't know Grant Cardone, he owns 15 companies that turnover $150 million per year and has a property portfolio surpassing $1.2 billion in value. I flew to Sydney to attend his Business Bootcamp earlier this year, I hadn't been following Grant much at the time but my partner Adrian had and he was all in. I thought to myself, I have nothing to lose, who knows what could show up for me. So, I invested in the $5,000 ticket, booked flights and the next week we were there. I'll admit, I felt very out of my depth in that room. Most people were millionaires and the two days were very business-focused on scaling and growing your business. In my head I kept thinking, I can't even finish my book, let alone think about scaling my business. But, something happened at the very end of the day. Grant asked the VIP tables for one key take-home from the day. He got to our table and my partner, Adrian, raised his hand to speak. As he gave his answer, something unexpected happened.

"What business to do run?" Grant asked.
"Ah, well, I'm at the beginning of my journey right now," he responded. *"I'm currently writing a book on leadership but I'm just starting."*
"Why the hell are you doing that, man!?" Grant asked.
Adrian froze, so I jumped in and tried to explain why we were both writing.
"We're both so passionate about our work and we're trying to write our books to help share our ideas with others"
Grant responds with.
"What the hell are you trying for? That's your problem. Why are you writing a book, when you should be finishing a book?"

Clearly seeing how stunned we were, Grant responded with, *"If you get your book done by Sunday, I'll promote it for you."*

I think me and Adrian were both stunned. In fact, he was ecstatic and I was about to burst into tears. I was terrified. Terrified of the little time we had, terrified of putting my work out there because it was so far from finished. I had just restarted the book for the fourth time, my ideas were everywhere and I had almost nothing to show for the three months of work I had dedicated. But, I also knew I would regret it for the rest of my life If I didn't accept his challenge. I mean, I had just paid this guy $5,000, I may as well take his advice and listen to what he had to say!

He did have a point, I was *trying* to do this write-a-book-thing. But I actually wasn't doing either. I was talking about pushing through roadblocks and having the courage to take risks, but I wasn't doing it myself.

Did I want to keep being Rebeccah, the girl who 'tried but never did,' or did I want to become Rebeccah Statham, the woman who took the challenge head-on and finished this book?

I knew the answer and I knew it was going to take everything I had. It would take letting go of being a perfectionist, and it would mean working harder than ever before. I knew deep down that this vision was so much bigger than my fears and that with Grants following of almost three people, who knew how many people would read my book and feel inspired to create change.

I didn't have time to step one foot in front of the other, I had no choice but to leap and figure out the "how" along the way. I had to wholeheartedly commit. And guess what? We did it. Me and my partner Adrian were lucky enough to meet an incredible publishing team, Dean Publishing who supported us and helped up to publish our books. We did not stop for 96 hours. But guess what? We did it. You're reading it now.

We all have choices in life, and we all have to make sacrifices. In order to be able to take action, you need to be able to decide which hard is going to be better for you.

Is stepping out of your comfort zone and trying new things your version of 'hard', or is sitting at home feeling lonely harder? Do you choose the hard of working in a career that doesn't inspire you for the next 40 years of your life? Do you choose the hard of grinding away after hours working on your side business? Is going to the gym hard, or is feeling uncomfortable in your skin harder because you don't exercise?

We all have a hard in our lives, it's just up to us to choose which hard we are willing to commit to.

It was a hard lesson for me to learn, but an incredibly important one as well.

Hopefully by this point of the book you're starting to see what's possible in your own life. Hopefully you've begun to build belief in your own abilities and you're opening up to all the opportunities around you. Because you can achieve whatever you want in this life. The fact that you're reading this book and looking to break free from your comfort zone is proof of that! You should be so proud of yourself. Igniting your spark takes belief. It takes courage and a willingness to step out of your comfort zone. But that's only half the battle.

At some point, you must take action. Real, tangible, committed action.

It takes more than just education, books, courses or seminars. You can watch motivational videos forever, but at the end of the day, we can't achieve our dreams without taking massive, bold, unapologetic action.

You might fail, but so what. You might also win big.

Gary Vaynerchuck, CEO of Vayner Media uses the analogy of doing push-ups. He says, "You can't read about push-ups, you gotta do them."

I too have been guilty of attending every personal development seminar I could get to, or listening to every podcast I could, or planning to get ready.

I thought that was enough to make things happen, but it wasn't. It never will be. Belief goes a long way, but action goes even further to building your dreams.

There's a saying I like to remind myself off as I go — "the obstacle is the way." I hadn't really understood it until recently, but I now realise that the only way to push through your obstacle, is to take action. Without committed action, you'll always play small.

So, the question is, what kind of hard will you commit to? Are you willing to take a risk, step out of your comfort zone and commit? You never know what magic could happen from taking a leap of faith.

"We delight in the beauty of the butterfly, but rarely admit the changes it has gone through to achieve that beauty."
Maya Angelou

BE UNAPOLOGETIC

There is really no other way to begin than to start with bold, unapologetic action. Don't wait for the approval of others, back yourself and go for it. There is always someone that has to be brave enough to take the first step forward.

Whatever path you choose, select it for yourself. Not what your parents told you you should do as you were growing up. Not what society tells you is the "right" way to do something. Not what anyone's opinions are. You need to do what ignites the spark inside of you, and be fearlessly unapologetic as you strive towards your dreams with committed action. Be proud of your choices and own them. It's empowering.

This is your life and only you get to decide what is right for you! Not everyone will understand your vision, it's not meant to be understood by everyone because that vision chose you. Be proud of whatever commitments you make today and know that you're making them for you. Be fearless, be courageous. And always, be unapologetic about your dreams.

People are going to tell you how they think you should

live your life, no matter what. You'll have haters, and you'll have doubters. So you need to remind yourself of what's important to you along the way. Positive self-talk is vital. People will always tell you how to conform, so it's up to you to choose how you live your own life, and be proud to do so.

Listen to the small voice inside your heart and forget about what other people say or think. Who cares?! This is your life, so go live it how you want! You were put on this planet to pave your own path, not copy someone else's. Use your voice, use your vision, and be unapologetic with your actions! Follow your heart. You've got this!

+++

"One of the greatest regrets in life is being what others would want you to be, rather than being yourself."
Shannon L. Alder

POWER OF IDEAS

Have you ever considered that ideas choose you? Or that your dreams and visions come to you for a reason?

In her book *Big Magic*, Elizabeth Gilbert talked about the topic of "ideas" — it impacted the way I appreciate and honour the dreams and ideas I will have forever. She says that "ideas are alive" and that they seek human collaborators on earth. These ideas know their worth and wish to be born into the world so they set off on an adventure to find the most willing person to collaborate with. Just as lightning chooses to strike through the best conductor, ideas are the same. The idea chooses the most efficient person to conduit the idea into the world, and then it will try and wave you down, get your attention and place clues in your way - but if you ignore the ideas, or take too long to act it will move onto someone else. I've had so many ideas that I ignored, and then later saw them popping up on Instagram, I thought, "I swear I had that thought a few years ago".

Has anything like this ever happened to you? Have you ever had an idea that you didn't act on and then out of nowhere someone else is doing the exact thing you wanted to do?

....

....

....

Don't be afraid to listen to your ideas. I believe they are there for a reason, although it doesn't mean you have to take action on all of your ideas. You are allowed to politely decline them, but always be grateful for having them. Just because you are capable of pursuing an idea doesn't mean you should always do it. Whenever you are unsure, connect back to your why statement. Does it align? If yes. Go for it. All in. If no. Say thank you to the idea but move on to the next.

I cannot recall the hours I have spent filling notebook after notebook with new ideas, companies I would one day start, bikini labels, silk-embellished crystal dresses I have drawn, jewellery labels that I have imagined. Most have stayed on paper, some I began planning and then stopped when I realised it wasn't in alignment with my why. It's okay to change your mind on things, because if you don't put the idea out into the world, someone else will. But make sure your reasons are valid!

The advice Gilbert gives for those seeking their ideas is to "Listen. Follow your curiosity. Ask questions. Sniff around. Remain open. Trust in the miraculous truth that new and marvellous ideas are looking for human collaborators every single day. Ideas of every kind are constantly galloping towards us constantly passing through us, constantly trying to get our attention. Let them know you're available. And for heavens sake, try not to miss the next one."

Remember that even though something may have been done before, it has never been done by you.

What ideas haven't left you... yet? How could you honour them and start taking action on them today?

....
....
....
....

"It is not true that people stop pursuing dreams because they grow old, they grow old because they stop pursuing dreams."
Gabriel García Márquez

GET IN THE ARENA.
BE BRAVE AND JUST DO IT.

"When we're defined by what people think, we lose the courage to be vulnerable. Therefore, we need to be selective about the feedback we let into our lives. For me, if you're not in the arena also getting your ass kicked, I'm not interested in your feedback."
Brene Brown

Imagine you're standing in the middle of a stadium surrounded by thousands of people looking down at you. They're all yelling at you, hurling down their own beliefs, stories and judgements at you.

"Just give up."

"You're not good enough."

"You can't do it."

You hear them all. They're quite the opinionated bunch. They have dreams just like you, but there's one huge difference. They're in the stands judging you, protected by the sea of people around them, where it's safe. They're not the ones on the field in the spotlight. They're not the ones stepping out of their comfort zones to do something great. It's scary, so they don't even try. They have potential just like you but they're frightened to walk out into the arena and risk being ridiculed, laughed at or failing.

The arena is where you go to take risks. It's where you go to step out of your comfort zone, and it's where you go to live a big life. The arena is scary, but it's the place for growth.

In his famous 1910 speech, 'Citizenship in a Republic' former US President, Theodore Roosevelt told an audience in the Grand Amphitheater at the University of Paris how he saw "the arena".

"It is not the critic who counts; not the man who points out how the strong man stumbles, or where the doer of deeds could have done them better. The credit belongs to the man who is actually in the arena, whose face is marred by dust and sweat and blood; who strives valiantly; who errs, who comes short again and again, because there is no effort without error and shortcoming; but who does actually strive to do the deeds; who knows great enthusiasms, the great devotions; who spends himself in a worthy cause; who at the best knows in the end the triumph of high achievement, and who at the worst, if he fails, at least fails while daring greatly, so that his place shall never be with those cold and timid souls who neither know victory nor defeat."

At the end of the day, if you don't take risks and commit to action, you'll end up like everybody else in the stands, playing small where it's safe. Those are the people who never truly understand what it takes to dare greatly and go all in. To realise their potential and in pursuit of their potential, ignite the spark inside of them. That's not for you, I know you are braver than that, I know you have the courage within you to do big and brave things with your life and I know you have a spark inside of you to share with the world.

It's easy to judge from the sidelines but it's hard to step into the arena and take action and that's what makes it worth it. Forget about those who criticise you for playing big and stepping out into the field. You're the brave one here, and the brave ones win! The spectators don't know about the courage it takes to step forward into the unknown, so disregard them. It's your arena, and they're only watching.

Igniting your spark and living your life to its fullest potential is to shine your light brightly out into this world. It's to be loud and fierce, even when you feel timid or shy. It's to step into the arena every single day and pave a new way forward for yourself. You were born for a reason, so make it happen. Turn those dreams into a reality.

There will always be people who try to dull your light, so it's up to each of us to remain courageous in the face of adversity. When someone tries to push you down, it's up to you to stand taller than before. It's up to you to be the gladiator in your own arena. Your job isn't to dim your shine in order to make others feel better about themselves. Your job is to light others up by being the best version of yourself that you can possibly be. Shine your light brighter than ever before and illuminate the world with your purpose. The very act of stepping into the arena makes you more courageous and successful than anyone on the sidelines. So, when you walk in, go all in. Don't hold back, overthink it or listen to the voices on the outside.

You don't have to be fearless to step into the arena, you just have to be willing.

I'm often scared and I don't think that will ever really go away. But I know I have to continue to push through, and continue to block out the doubt if I want to be great.

If I succumb to the pressure, I'll never be able to help people around the world to ignite their own spark. It would be selfish of me to dim my light and conform to the expectations of others, just as it would be selfish of you to keep your light inside of you only. Let it out, and become a beacon of hope for the world like you know you can become!

Life is to be lived to the fullest, so dive into the depths of who you really are and share that gorgeous gift of yours with the world. Become the person you were truly meant to be. You won't ever fail by giving it your all. You will transform. You will grow. You will redefine yourself and you'll create something extraordinary.

You'll never know what could have been unless you truly push yourself to go all in and become vulnerable. Leave it all out in the arena, where there's nowhere to hide. Show your truth and your realness, that is what will separate you from everyone else.

There's no other you in this world, so your superpower is being your unique self, regardless of what others think or say. You can learn any skill if you are willing enough to take committed action, and you can become anyone you want to become if you truly work hard enough for it.

Remember that everything is learnable, and most of the questions we ask we already know the answers to. We just have to push past our own blockages and believe in ourselves. It's that simple.

You're unique in this world, so don't let anyone else dictate how to live your life. It's yours, and yours only. Only you know what's right. Only you can ignite your spark and discover what it takes to live in your zone of genius. Give yourself permission to chase your dreams and make room for the impossible to show up in your life.

I want to leave you with one final thought.

There's no perfect moment and no time will ever be 'just right' to take action on your dreams. 'The right time' does not exist. All you have is the moment right now, where you decide to listen to your heart and chase your dreams. Whatever it is that lights you up — chase that. It will bring you more joy and excitement than you could ever imagine.

Challenge the norm, and become an exception to the rule.

You can't erase your past, but from this moment onwards, you can rewrite your future.

Let go of what no longer serves you. Live like you've never lived before.

You're capable of doing incredible things in this world. Now is your time, so go make it happen.

I believe in you. Now it's time for you to believe in who you are. It's time to *Ignite Your Spark*.

"You have to find what sparks a light in you so that you, in your own way, can illuminate the world"
Oprah Winfrey

IGNITE YOUR SPARK
INTERVIEWS WITH REBECCAH

Michael Ellis
Life Enthusiast | Conscious culture creator | Human Behaviour Expert | Writer at Lonely Planet

Rebeccah: What advice would you give to someone that has lost their spark "growing up"?
Michael: It's all just a story. And you're the author. Write a new story.

Rebeccah: If you could wave a magic wand and instil one belief into every human being, what would that be?
Michael: That you are worthy. It's not something you need to earn – you were born, you're alive, you're worthy. Now, go do something magnificent!

Rebeccah: What does living a life that excites you mean to you?
Michael: I consider it a privilege to live a life and so I want to make the most of it. I want to enjoy my life, to have fun, to explore and experience meaning. And to share and support

others to do the same – this is what living a life that excites me looks like.

+++

Alexie O'Brien
COO Tell me Baby | Non-Executive Director | Board advisor | Passionate game-changer

Rebeccah: Think back to your younger self, when everything and anything seemed possible. What is one piece of advice your five-year-old self would tell you and the people reading this?
Alexie: I would tell my five-year-old self that you are worthy, and you are enough. I would tell her that you can achieve things and be proud of yourself, but take time to enjoy life and the process. Smell the roses, enjoy the view on the climb and don't worry what other people think so much. The constant striving for achievements, accolades and validation from others is just not necessary. You add value, you are worthy and self- love is not selfish.

Rebeccah: If you could wave a magic wand and instil one belief into every human being, what would that be?
Alexie: You are bigger, brighter, smarter, more compassionate than you could ever possibly imagine. Live into your potential, not your constraints.

Rebeccah: What are your thoughts on fear and failure? And do you think they play an important part in our lives?
Alexie: Oh absolutely! Fear is there to remind us that we have a choice. We can let it stop us and limit us, or we can grow from it. Failure is part of that. Failure is a necessary part of growth.

However it needs to be couple with awareness and reflection. Failure only serves us when we learn from it, not when we let it defeat, deflate and constrain us. It is when we are unstoppable – in spite of the fear, or failure that we will be our best selves.

Rebeccah: Why are we so many of us scared of living a big purposeful life?

Alexie: Many reasons - sometimes it is because we are scared of failure. It could be a fear of what happens if we succeed or maybe we are worried about judgement from others. We are afraid to disappoint people and not live into others expectations of us. Sometimes it is because we just don't know what that is and how big is big, what is purposeful. We don't all need to be Rosa Parks, or Rosie Batty to live a purposeful life. The key is what is YOUR big purposeful life. And then get out of your own way and go live it.

Rebeccah: Why do you think most people settle for mediocrity as opposed to stepping out "into the arena" in pursuit of a life that excites them and ignites their fullest human potential?

Alexie: It is easiest to stay put than to step out onto a ledge and risk things. It is scary and unknown with no guarantees of success. I think also because people aren't connected to a Why – small or big that inspires them to do whatever it takes. No MATTER what.

Anything is possible from here.

THANK YOU

Thank you to my beautiful family for teaching me courage, strength, love, kindness, forgiveness, gratitude and for always encouraging me to go out there in the world, follow my heart and shine my light bright, no matter what darkness was around me at the time.

Thank you to my partner Adrian, for your love, patience, strength, determination and support.

Thank you to my friends for being my family when I had none around. No matter how short, distant or long our friendship is, I value and love you all so much.

Thank you to Dean Publishing for your time, commitment and believing that this was possible. For making this book and this story come into the world.

Thank you to Grant Cardone for challenging me to write this book.

And all the other previous mentors that have pushed me to think big.

And thank you, to YOU — for reading this and taking a chance on me. I hope you go out there and shine your light bright into the world.

Lightning Source UK Ltd.
Milton Keynes UK
UKHW020627201119
353895UK00013B/1137/P